# ANCIENT SCROLLS

*The Lerner Archaeology Series*

DIGGING UP THE PAST:

AN INTRODUCTION TO ARCHAEOLOGY

# ANCIENT SCROLLS

by Michael Avi-Yonah

retold for young readers by Richard L. Currier

Lerner Publications Company ● Minneapolis, Minnesota, USA.

ACKNOWLEDGMENT

The illustrations are reproduced through the courtesy of: p. 9 Department of Antiquities &
Museums, Ministry of Culture, Israel; École Biblique et Archéologique Française; p. 11;
15; 16; 26; 51; 56; 57; 61; 64; 76 The British Museum, London; p. 14; 22; 24; 35; 38; 39;
87; 91 Department of Antiquities & Museums, Ministry of Culture, Israel; p. 19; 33; 53;
58 Hirmer Photoarchiv, München; p. 23 The Oriental Institute, University of Chicago;
p. 34 Biblioteca Medicea Laurenziana, Firenze; Dr. Pineider, Firenze; p. 44; 81; 88; 89; 90
The Shrine of the Book, Israel Museum, Jerusalem; p. 47 Yad Ben-Zvi, Jerusalem; p. 50
Lowie Museum of Anthropology, University of California, Berkeley. p. 55 Universitets-
biblioteket i Oslo; p. 59; 62 Bayerische Staatsbibliothek, München; p. 60 The Dumbarton
Oaks Collection, Washington, D.C.; p. 73; 74; 75 Biblioteca Ambrosiana, Milano.


Photography adviser: Irit Salmon

## Designed by Ofra Kamar

First published in the United States of America 1974
by Lerner Publications Company, Minneapolis, Minnesota.

International Standard Book Number: 0–8225–0827–3.
Library of Congress Catalog Card Number: 72–10792.

Printed in Israel and bound in the United States.

# CONTENTS

# I  THE EARLIEST WRITING MATERIALS

Can you imagine a world in which no one knows how to read or write? Strange as that may seem, it was a reality for most of the hundreds of thousands of years that human beings have lived on the earth. After the first cities appeared, however, people needed some way of keeping track of the great number of things and people that were crowded together in the city's many houses, storerooms, workshops, and palaces. The early city dwellers invented marks or signs to represent the things and people they wanted to keep track of, and this is how the idea of writing began.

Once people could read and write, it was not necessary to depend on a person's memory to preserve knowledge. Information could be written down, and it would be preserved exactly, as long as the material it was written on survived. In fact, some of the earliest writings of mankind have survived into our own time, and they are now kept carefully guarded in museums. Many of these ancient writings would look like little more than strange patterns and designs to most of us, but they can be understood by scholars and scientists who have spent many years studying them and learning how to read them. This book is about the kinds of writing done by people who lived in Europe and the Near East hundreds and even thousands of years ago. It is also about the efforts that have been made in our time to find, preserve, and understand the ancient writings that have survived.

The oldest examples of writing come from two places in the Middle East, not too far from the ancient city of Jerusalem. One is Mesopotamia, an ancient land which now includes the modern country of Iraq. The keepers of Mesopotamian temples made careful records of the property belonging to the temple sanctuaries. In Egypt, special inscribed seals were placed on property belonging to the Pharaohs and their families.

As writing became more common, ancient people discovered that there were a variety of animal, vegetable, and mineral materials that were suitable for writing, and that each kind of material could serve a particular kind of purpose. The perishable but inexpensive materials could be used for the less important writings, and the more expensive and more permanent materials could be saved for important documents and records.

## Stone

The schoolboys of ancient Greece used small tablets of a flat, gray stone called "slate" as exercise books. The dark gray blackboards in our older schoolrooms are actually large, flat slate stones that have been carefully cut and smoothed for writing. We use chalk (another mineral substance) to write on slate, but the Greek schoolboys scratched their letters on the slate with a sharp point. In general, though, writing on stone was so slow and difficult that it was used only on monuments meant for public display, such as statues, temples, or pyramids.

Writing on stone was usually done by cutting the letters or signs into the surface of the stone with a ham-

mer and chisel. Most people found that the most comfortable way of doing this was by holding the chisel in the left hand and striking it with a hammer held in the right hand. Since the hammer was striking from

A Roman military diploma, inscribed on a bronze tablet

right to left, it was easiest to carve the signs from right to left. The Semitic languages — which include Hebrew and Arabic — still use this ancient way of writing from right to left.

A copper scroll found near the Dead Sea

## Metal

Although some of the most important ancient scrolls ever found are made of metal, very few writings on metal have survived to the present day. Metal was much more expensive than other materials, and it was therefore used less often. In addition, there was always the temptation to melt down the metal sheets or plates and use the metal for making weapons, or even money. But metal was impressive, beautiful, and very durable, and a number of noteworthy examples of metal writing still exist.

Some of the rich and powerful nobles of ancient times used sheets of gold and silver for writing. Gold was also used in Jerusalem for keeping some of the records of the Second Temple, although bronze and copper were used more often. In fact, bronze and copper were so easily stored and lasted so well that most of the archives — or government records — of ancient Greece and Rome consisted of row upon row of bronze tablets upon which official treaties and decrees were carefully inscribed. Soldiers dismissed honorably from the Roman army after long service had their citizenship rights recorded on small bronze tablets called "diplomas." Many of these diplomas have been found, and have provided us with a great deal of information about the military units of those times.

Scrolls made of copper have been found in a cave near the ruin of Qumran close to the Dead Sea. From certain marks on the scrolls, archaeologists conclude that they were once fastened to the wall as tablets; thus, they seem to have once been part of a permanent record of some kind. These Qumran scrolls are something of a mystery, however, because they describe a fantastic list of treasures. It seems strange that a description of such fabulous riches should have been displayed on a wall, and for this reason some scientists doubt that this treasure ever really existed. Others, however, argue that if there were no such treasure, why would anyone have taken the trouble to describe it in such an expensive and durable material as copper?

The ancients also wrote on sheets of lead. This heavy, dull metal was used for a special and sinister purpose: putting a curse on someone or something. The curse would be written on a lead tablet. This object,

Buddhist writings on palm wood

A wooden advertisement board, or album

called an "execration tablet," was supposed to have a magical influence over the person or thing that the curse was supposed to affect. It is interesting to note that while most of the metals used for writing are harmless, lead is quite poisonous. As far as we know, however, the ancients were unaware of lead's poisonous properties.

It was slow and difficult work inscribing words and symbols on stone or metal, and the heavy scrolls and tablets could take up a great deal of space. For these reasons, the ancients more often used softer, lighter, and cheaper materials, such as wood, wax, pottery, and clay.

## Wood

The most extensive use of wood as a writing material occurred in the Orient, where the Buddhists collected entire libraries of writings on light palm wood. The Greeks and Romans never used wooden tablets in such quantity, but they did use whitened boards for displaying important public notices. This board, called an "album," could be whitewashed again and again so that the old notices could be covered as they expired and replaced with new ones as the occasion demanded. The famous inscription "Jesus of Nazareth King of the Jews" was written on a wooden tablet. The inscription was repeated in Latin, Greek, and Hebrew (or Aramaic) on a tablet set over the cross of Jesus at the time of the Crucifixion. Of course, wood decays quickly when it becomes damp, and few of these wooden tablets have lasted into our own times. Except for countries such as Egypt, where there is little rainfall, wood is not a permanent material.

## Wax

One the more convenient writing materials of the ancient world was made by covering wooden tablets with a layer of wax. The wood gave the tablet strength and firmness, and the wax provided a smooth, soft surface which could be easily scratched with a pointed instrument. These tablets were sometimes fastened together by a ring on one side, so that they could be turned, like the pages

Wax tablet joined together to form a codex

of a book. The Romans called such a group of tablets a "codex" (plural, "codices"), and this word later became the common name for a book composed of many sheets. Wax tablets were used for notices and for other kinds of temporary writings, since (unlike stone or metal writings) they could not be expected to last indefinitely. Sometimes even legal and financial records were made on wax tablets: at Pompeii (a Roman city near Naples, Italy), contracts for loans and other banking records have been found that were written on wax. Once the loans had been paid or the transactions concluded, the contracts were no longer needed and could be erased.

The ancients wrote on their wax tablets with a special tool called a "stylus." One end of the stylus was sharply pointed and was used for writing. The other end was broad and flat and was used for erasing, which was done by simply smoothing out the surface that had been written upon. Our word for the way in which a person writes — what we call a person's "style" — comes from the name of this ancient writing instrument. Because it was so easy to erase wax tablets, they were the most common notebooks of the ancient world.

Stylus used for writing on wax tablets

A somewhat gruesome story about wax tablets is told of the emperor Caligula, who ruled the Roman Empire for only four years but who quickly earned a reputation for being one of the most cruel and blood-thirsty of all Roman emperors. Caligula had many people put to death during his reign, and — according to the story — he instructed his secretaries to use two wax tablet notebooks to record the names of those who were to die. One tablet was made with red wax, and on this, Caligula's secretaries were to note the names of those who would die by the sword. The other tablet was made with black wax, and on this were written the names of those who were to die by poison. Of course, Caligula and other less bloodthirsty rulers constantly used regular wax tablets for purposes that were not quite as ghastly as this.

## Ostraca

Ostraca are pieces of broken pottery, and ancient people must have had a tremendous supply of this material. In our time, most vessels and containers — such as bottles, jars, and cooking pots — are made of plastic, metal, or glass, but in ancient times these common objects (and many other things as well) were made of pottery. Pottery is easily broken, however, and the broken pieces of pottery vessels — called "potsherds" — tended to accumulate. The ancients used these potsherds in much the same way that we use scrap paper: for letters, short messages, receipts, or anything of a temporary nature that would eventually be thrown away. A person would simply select a potsherd of the right size and write the message onto the surface of the pottery.

Although ostraca were meant to be temporary, they proved to be practically indestructible. Tens of thousands of them have been found in archaeological excavations all over the world, and they have provided us with much useful information about ancient life. Hebrew ostraca of biblical times have been found which have improved our understanding of the Hebrew script and which contain information about the political and economic life of those times. One piece from Israel's Negev desert,

A Hebrew ostracon from the sixth century B.C.

for example, recorded that a certain man had done his civic duty by laboring for one day to clean the public water reservoirs. Great numbers of ostraca have also been found in Egypt, where they were once used for tax receipts. Since taxes had to be paid every year, these receipts did not have to be kept for very long. When they were no longer needed, they were simply thrown on the rubbish heap, where archaeologists of another age might find them, hundreds or even thousands of years later.

## Clay

Clay tablets were probably invented by the Sumerians of southern Babylonia, who built one of the oldest civilizations on earth. The Sumerians first used clay tablets to

A very ancient example of cuneiform writing

keep records of temple property, but clay tablets eventually came to be used in all parts of the ancient world. At one time, even the Pharaohs of Egypt used clay tablets for correspondence.

Clay tablets usually consisted of two parts: an inner core on which the message was written, and an outer layer of clay which covered the core and on which the message was repeated. When a person wanted to read the tablet, he normally consulted only this outer layer. If the tablet had been damaged, however, or for some other reason was impossible to read, then this outer layer could be broken and the original record beneath it could be read.

Ancient people wrote on clay tablets while the clay was still soft by making small triangular impressions

A cuneiform tablet from ancient Babylon

with a sharp, wedge-shaped instrument of wood or metal. This is called "cuneiform writing," from the Latin word *cuneus,* or "wedge." At first, these little wedge-shaped marks were arranged to form a crude picture of the object they were meant to represent. But as time passed these pictures were slightly rearranged and simplified, until many of them were no longer pictures at all but strange-looking symbols that had to be memorized to be understood. (Chinese writing also developed in this way — from pictures to signs.) Cuneiform writing could be done in any direction: right, left, up, or down, as long as the signs were arranged in the proper order.

When the clay tablet was finished, it was placed in an oven and baked until it was dry and hard. This hardened clay proved to be so durable that many of the tablets are still in excellent condition, three or four thousand years later. Clay tablets were so widely used, and they lasted so well, that they have been found in thousands of archaeological excavations in Iraq (where the Sumerians lived), in Israel, and in many other countries. All in all, there are about a million of these tablets safely stored in museums, and there are certain to be many more still waiting to be found.

Each of these early writing materials was useful for a certain purpose, and they must all have been more or less satisfactory to ancient people or their use would never have become so widespread. But these materials all had the disadvantage of being heavy and bulky. This was not especially important if you only needed to write a few sentences. But if you wanted to write down dozens of songs or poems, make a list of thousands of items in a palace storeroom, or write down the story of an important conquest by a great army, you would need a large number of heavy, bulky tablets. All together, the tablets would make a large, heavy, and clumsy pile of material. It would be difficult to store, and it would be even more difficult to take from one place to another. For these reasons, the ancient world came to rely more and more on a cheap, light, and compact material called "papyrus."

## II PAPYRUS SCROLLS

In the hot, humid marshlands of northern Egypt, where the Nile River empties into the Mediterranean Sea, there grows a tall marsh plant called "papyrus." The papyrus plant was so important to the people of ancient Egypt that it came to be used as a symbol for Lower Egypt, just as the bald eagle is used as a symbol for the United States of America today. Various parts of the papyrus plant were used for fuel, food, medicine, clothes, rugs, sails, ropes, and even for a kind of chewing gum. But to most of the ancient world, the most important use of papyrus was in making the world's first cheap, light, and compact writing material. From the word "papyrus" has come the name for our own favorite writing material — paper. Both papyrus and paper are made of vegetable material that has been pressed into thin, flat sheets.

### Making Papyrus

To prepare papyrus for writing, the outer bark was first removed from the thick lower part of the stem. Then the inside core of the plant was peeled off in strips, and the strips were laid out on a flat surface, side by side, to form a sheet. When this was done, a second layer of strips was laid out on top of the first one, but with the strips running at right angles to the ones beneath. The two layers of papyrus strips were then beaten with a hammer until they had fused into a single sheet. The result was a strong, flat writing surface with vertical lines on one side and horizontal lines on the other, all formed by the edges of the strips. The sheet was then dried, cut to a standard size, and smoothed with a light powdery stone called "pumice."

Single sheets of papyrus could be used for letters or notes, and many sheets could be glued end to end to make a long scroll, upon which a book could be written. The scroll was then rolled up with the horizontal lines on the inside and the vertical lines on the outside. Most of these rolls were a standard size, consisting of 20 papyrus sheets each. But there were larger rolls, some as long as 133 feet — almost half the length of a football field!

Papyrus was used in Palestine from the time the Jews first settled there, and parts of the Bible might have been first written down on papyrus scrolls. We do know that the governments of ancient Israel and Nabataea (a small kingdom in what is now part of Jordan) used papyrus for their official documents. Archaeologists have found evidence that these documents were rolled up and fastened with a clay seal upon which a mark or design had been stamped. These papyrus scrolls could have told us much about the history of these ancient societies, but they have entirely disappeared. All that is left are the small clay seals with their interesting designs, yet we should be grateful even for these.

The Egyptians used an enormous amount of papyrus for records and documents: one record tells us that in the third century B.C., a certain Egyptian official used 434 rolls of papyrus in only 33 days. This is truly an amazing amount, but it is possible that many of these expensive rolls were stolen or simply taken by dishonest officials.

Sadly, the quality of the Egyptian papyrus declined as time passed. Papyrus from the 14th to the 11th centuries B.C. is fine and even, but that from the third and second centuries B.C. is heavier and thicker. Papyrus from the years following the time of Christ is the clumsiest and coarsest of all.

*Writing on Papyrus*

The standard rolls of papyrus were each about 35 feet long, and this fact explains why certain books

An Egyptian scribe

This Roman painting shows a man holding a scroll. Two Egyptian gods stand on either side of him.

of the Old Testament (such as Samuel, Kings, and Chronicles) were divided into two parts. One papyrus roll was not long enough to contain each of these books, but if the rolls were made much longer than this standard size, they would have been too large and too heavy to handle comfortably. Therefore, each book was put on two separate rolls. On the other hand, the 12 small books of the Prophets were put together on a single roll, even though they are all quite different from each other. The same thing happened with the *Odyssey* and the *Iliad,* the two great works of the ancient Greek poet Homer. When these works were written down, each was divided into 24 books, each book the length of one standard papyrus roll.

The Egyptians wrote on papyrus with a reed dipped in ink. The Greeks, who eventually began to use papyrus themselves, improved on this system by using reeds of hard material which could be split in two, like the tip of a fountain pen. The ink was made of lampblack — the sooty substance which sometimes rises from the tip of a candle flame — mixed with water and the sticky sap of certain plants. This ink was incredibly durable, and papyrus scrolls many thousands of years old can still be read without difficulty. Occasionally, however, a metallic substance that was used in the ink corroded the papyrus.

In general, the side of the papyrus sheet with the horizontal lines was meant to be written on first, although the reverse side was equally suitable for writing. The front side was often used for official documents, leaving the reverse side blank. Then, when the official archives became stuffed to overflowing with old documents, the rolls were sold as waste paper, and people could still use the blank reverse side for notes, messages, and records.

From Egypt, writing on papyrus spread to Phoenicia (on the eastern shore of the Mediterranean), and the Phoenicians brought it to Greece. Strangely enough, the word "Bible" in our language comes from this trading of papyrus from the Phoenicians to the Greeks. The Phoenicians shipped papyrus out of one particular Phoenician city, which the Greeks called "Byblos." In time, the Greeks began calling the papyrus itself "byblos" too. Since the Greeks made their books out of papyrus, they eventually began to call their books "biblos." In the end, this Greek name for *book* was applied to what the Europeans considered

An ancient ink pot

The writing equipment of an Egyptian scribe

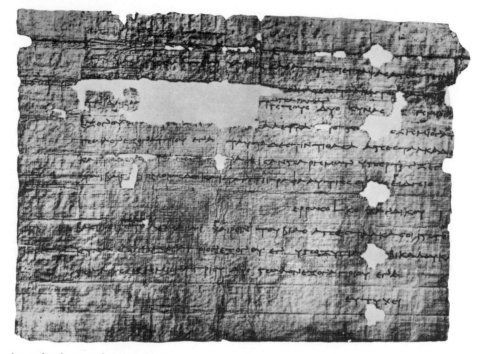

An ancient letter, written on papyrus

the most important book of all: the Holy Scriptures.

Once a roll of papyrus was filled with writing, it was normally kept safe in one of two ways. Some rolls were placed on open shelves in libraries, and each roll was provided with a small tag for identification. Others were stored in special boxes, which held 10 rolls apiece. While the ancients may have found this a useful method for storing papyrus scrolls, it has had some unfortunate consequences for us. Some of the ancient writings that have survived are miss-ing large sections of 10 books each, while other groups of 10 books are intact. Apparently, entire boxes of scrolls were lost at once, while other groups of 10 have survived.

*The Surviving Papyrus Scrolls*

Although most of the countries that border the Mediterranean are warm and dry most of the year, there is a rainy season for three or four months every winter. In this damp weather, papyrus manuscripts quick-ly decayed. Thus, despite the fact that papyrus was the most common

A library of scrolls. Notice the tags attached to most of the scrolls

writing material of ancient times, little of it has survived to the present time. The only place in Europe where papyrus scrolls survived from ancient times was in the old Roman city of Herculaneum, near present-day Naples. In the year A.D. 79, Herculaneum was destroyed by a sudden eruption of the volcano Vesuvius. An entire library of papyrus scrolls, buried for many centuries beneath a thick layer of volcanic ash, miraculously survived. But this preservation of papyrus was a lucky accident. Not just anywhere can you count on the convenient eruption of a nearby volcano!

Outside of Europe, the largest number of ancient papyrus scrolls have been found in Lower Egypt, where the dry desert climate preserved all perishable materials — including wood and papyrus — as long as they were sufficiently far from the waters of the Nile. In the centuries that have passed since ancient times, some parts of the Nile Valley dried up. Areas that had once been fertile farmland turned into deserts, and the towns in those areas were

A work of ancient Greek literature on a papyrus scroll

abandoned. The rubbish heaps of these ruined towns proved to contain many ancient artifacts, and in the 19th century people began to dig for objects that could be sold to dealers in antiquities. One of the things they unearthed was papyrus scrolls — in enormous quantities.

At first, the value of this material was not understood. There is even a story that the dealers sometimes burned the sheets of papyrus, just to enjoy the pleasant aroma! In time, however, as these scrolls came to the attention of scholars and archaeologists, their true value came to be understood. From 1870 on, the rubbish heaps of certain towns and villages in Lower Egypt became our main source of papyrus scrolls. At one site, archaeologists found a heap of papyrus so thick that it took 12 workers several days just to dig through it. During a single day's work at that site, 36 baskets of papyrus scrolls were unearthed. At another site, the English archaeologist Sir Flinders Petrie discovered mummy cases made out of sheets of papyrus. A few years later it was found that some of the crocodile mummies were also stuffed with papyrus. (Crocodiles were considered sacred animals in that part of Egypt and were often prepared for burial according to a special ritual.)

*Right:* Ancient Greek writing

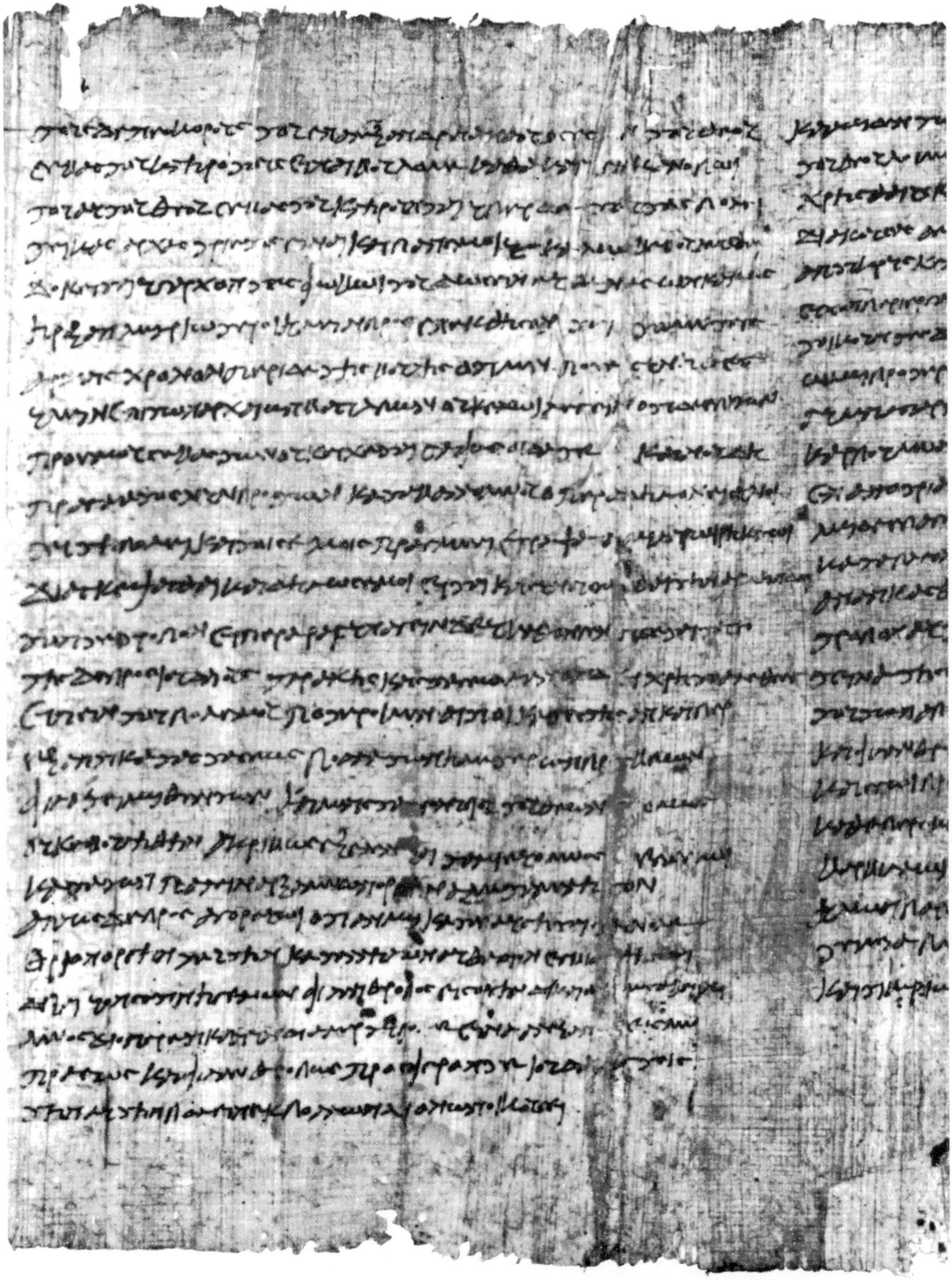

ΑΠΟΓΗϹΕΠΙΘΑΜΑΙΟΥϹ
ΗΚΑΙΜΕΙΖΟΝΑϹΡΙΖΑΝ
ΠΑΡΑΠΛΗϹΙΑΝΤΗΙΟ
ϹΜΥΡϹΙΝΗΙΜΕΙΖΟ
ΝΑΔΕΚΑΙΕΥΩΔΗΚΑ
ΩΤΕΡΑΝ·ΦΥΕΤΑΙΕΝ
ΤΟΠΟΙϹΟΡΙΝΟΙϹΔΥΝΑ
ΜΙΝΔΕΕΧΕΙΗΡΙΖΑΠΙ
ΝΟΜΕΝΗΔΡΑΧΜΩΝ
ΕΞΠΛΗΘΟϹΜΕΤΑΟΙ
ΝΟΥΓΛΥΚΕΟϹ·ΒΟΗ
ΘΕΙΝΤΑΙϹΔΥϹΤΟΚΟΥ
ϹΑΙϹΚΑΙϹΤΡΑΓΓΟΥ
ΡΙΩϹΙΝΑΓΡΕΙΑϹΚΑΙΑΙΜΑ
ϹΦΝΟΕΙΔΕϹ·ΟΙΔΕΟΥΠΙ
ΤΑΛΟΝ·ΟΙΔΕΧΑΜΑΙΔΑ
ΦΝΗΝ·ΟΙΔΕΠΕΠΛΟΝ
ΚΑΛΟΥϹΙΘΑΜΝΙϹΚΟϹ
ΕϹΤΙΠΗΧΕΩϹΤΟΥΦΟϹ
ΕΧΩΝΚΛΑΔΟΥϹΠΟΛΛΟΥϹ
ΚΑΙΠΑΝΤΩΔΕΙϹΠΡΟϹ
ΤΩΑΝΩΘΕΝΗΜΙϹΥ
ϹΦΥΛΛΟΦΟΡΟΥϹ·ϹΡΛΟΙ
ΘΕΔΕΠΕΡΙΤΑϹΡΑΒΔΟΥϹ
ΧΛΙϹΧΡΟϹ·ΤΕΧΥΡΟϹΦΥ
ΛΛΑΔΑΦΝΗϹΕΟΙΚΟΤΑ·
ΜΑΛΑΚΩΤΕΡΑΔΕΚΑΙ
ΧΥΡΩΤΕΡΑ·ΟΥΚΕΥΚΛΑ
ϹΤΑΔΑΚΝΟΝΤΑΚΑΙΠΥ
ΡΟΥϹΙΝΤΑΤΟϹΤΟΜΑΚΑΙΦΑΡΥΓΓΑ·ΑΝΘΟϹΑϹΥ
ΙΚΑΚΑΡΠΟΝΔΕΜΕΛΑΝΑΟΤΑΝΠΕΠΑΝΘΗ·
ΡΙΖΑΑΧΡΙΟϹ·ΦΥΕΤΑΙΕΝΟΡΙΝΟΙϹΤΟΠΟΙϹ·
ΑΓΡΙΑϹΤΟΦΥΛΛΟΝΑΥΤΟΥΞΗΡΟΝΠΙΝΕ
ΑΡΟΝΠΟΘΕΝΚΑΤΑΚΟΙΛΙΑΝΦΛΕΓΜΑΤΩ
ΔΗ·ΚΙΝΕΙΚΑΙΕΜΕΤΟΥϹΚΑΘΜΗΝΑ

Among the immense quantities of papyrus that were unearthed in Lower Egypt, some important literary works have been found. Most of these are the works of Greek authors, since this part of Egypt was strongly influenced by the ancient Greeks, especially in the centuries just before the birth of Christ. Poetry, famous speeches, and important legal documents have all been found among the Egyptian papyrus scrolls.

Papyrus scrolls have also been found in Persia and Iraq. Today the search for scrolls continues in these places and elsewhere. In all, archaeologists have unearthed almost 700 texts of the Greek poet Homer, as well as dozens of plays by ancient dramatists. Some of these plays were thought to have been lost forever, and others had been so long forgotten that modern scholars never even knew they existed. In addition, the hundreds of letters and official documents that have been found tell us much about the economic and political life of ancient times.

## Understanding Papyrus Scrolls

Scholars and scientists are faced with several problems in their efforts to understand these ancient papyrus scrolls. First, the scrolls themselves are often difficult to read. The clerks

who wrote or copied them were not always careful and they sometimes wrote in a hurry, especially when dealing with business matters. When they wrote in Greek or Latin, they did not print the letters separately and distinctly but rather used a running script which is sometimes very difficult to decipher. Second, the scrolls are often in poor physical condition: they may be badly torn, stained, and even decayed. Third, most groups of papyrus scrolls are only partly preserved. The ancient archives have been scattered, and sometimes different parts of the same text have been purchased by different museums and may no longer even be in the same part of the world.

Another type of problem concerns the interpretation of the manuscripts. Even when they can be read, scholars may disagree about their meaning or true importance. This problem is made even more difficult by the fact that almost nothing has survived from some parts of the world and from some periods of history, while great quantities of material may have survived from certain other times and places. Thus in some cases, we have knowledge of the tiniest details of government activities. We know, for example, that in the second century

*Left:* An ancient example of a Greek manuscript

B.C., in an obscure settlement called Cerceosiris, in Egypt, the village scribe was unable to add correctly! In other cases, we know almost nothing. The great royal capitals of Alexandria and Thebes, for example, have left us no records at all. The result is that the information we do have presents a very one-sided picture, in which many towns and cities seem, from our point of view, more important than they really were in ancient times. Therefore, we must be very careful about what conclusions we draw from the large but often confusing mass of papyrus scrolls which have survived from ancient times.

The papyrus scrolls that have been found are only a tiny fraction of the scrolls that once existed, for papyrus was the most common writing material of antiquity. The great library of Alexandria in Egypt alone once contained about 400,000 papyrus scrolls! Part of this library was destroyed during the first century B.C., when Cleopatra, the daughter of the king of Egypt, seized power with the help of the Roman general Julius Caesar. At a later period in Egyptian history, the rest of this great library was burned. As time passed, papyrus became increasingly scarce, although as late as the 11th century A.D. it was still being used by the pope's scribes and secretaries in Rome. Even in Egypt itself, the papyrus plant is now nearly extinct.

## III  PARCHMENT SCROLLS

As papyrus disappeared, ancient people gradually came to depend on parchment, a writing material made from the skins of animals. Parchment was first used nearly 2,000 years before Christ, but for a long time it was not nearly as common as papyrus. As the centuries passed, however, parchment grew more and more important until, by the Middle Ages, it had replaced papyrus in common use. Parchment remained the principal writing material of the Old World until the introduction of paper (a Chinese invention). It is the only writing material of ancient times which is still in use today (college diplomas and copies of famous historical documents are sometimes printed on parchment).

*Making Parchment*

Both leather and parchment are made from animal skins, but they are prepared by different methods. In both cases, the skins are washed, soaked in water, cleaned of all flesh and hair, and smoothed carefully. At this point, however, the skins that are to become leather are soaked again in a solution containing tannin, a substance made from the bark of certain trees. Over a period of several weeks, these skins gradually turn into leather. For parchment, however, the skins are not soaked in tannin but are instead stretched tight and left to dry. The result is a hard, flexible sheet, like a piece of thin, strong cardboard. This sheet is then rubbed with chalk and pumice stone to make it smooth and white. The irregular edges are trimmed off, and the result is parchment, ready for writing. Most parchment has always been made of the skins of sheep and goats, although the skins of calves and kids are used to make a particularly fine grade of parchment called "vellum."

*The Use of Parchment*

The oldest writing on animal skin we know of is a roll that is now kept in Berlin, Germany. It is said to come from the 12th Dynasty of ancient Egypt, nearly 4,000 years ago. Writing on leather skins was also done by the early Assyrians (who lived in present-day Iraq) in the 13th century B.C. According to the ancient historian Herodotus, the Persians, who were neighbors of the Assyrians, used "royal hides" for their historical records, but we do not know if Herodotus was referring to leather or parchment. The Hebrews and Assyrians of the eighth century B.C., however, are among the first people who are definitely known to have used parchment. Some of their parchment scrolls have survived to the present day.

During the centuries between this early date and the birth of Christ, papyrus was normally used for temporary purposes, such as keeping administrative records, while parchment came to be commonly used for writings of a permanent nature. Writings of great literary or religious importance, such as the scrolls of the Law or the sayings of the Prophets, had to be written on a durable material, and the ancients turned to parchment for this purpose.

The Bible contains proof of this early use of parchment, in a vivid passage from the book of Jeremiah, Chapter 36. In the biblical story, King Jehojakim sent Yehudi, his secretary, to fetch the scroll which contained Jeremiah's words. The Bible continues:

> ... and Yehudi read in the ears of the king and it came to pass when Yehudi had read three or four leaves he [the king] cut with it a penknife and he cast it into the fire that was on the hearth.

The story continues until the whole scroll was destroyed. If Jeremiah's words had been written on a papyrus scroll, the king could easily have torn it with his hands. Or the king could have thrown the entire scroll into the fire at once; papyrus burns as easily as wood or paper, and it would quickly have been consumed by the flames. But since the king had to cut the scroll with a pen knife and burn it one piece at a time, it must have been made of a strong material that was difficult to burn.

*Right:* An Egyptian scribe

*Overleaf left:* A scribe of the Middle Ages

*Overleaf right:* Pieces of glass from the fourth century, decorated with gold. Notice the rolled-up scrolls in the drawings

CODICIBVS SACRIS HOSTILI CLADE PERVSTIS
ESDRA DO FERVENS HOC REPARAVIT OPVS

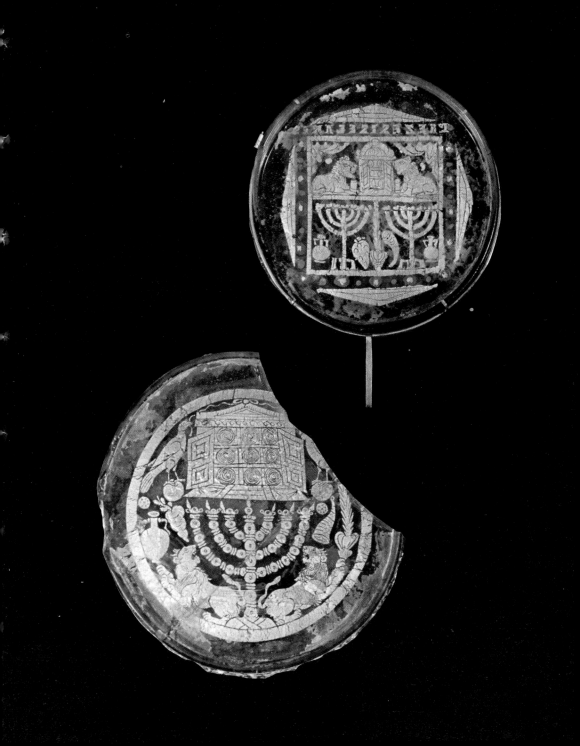

Lucas sirus·natoe anthiocensis·arte medic⁹·discipulus apostoloz·postea paulū secut⁹ vsq ad confessioneₑ ei⁹ seruiens dño sine crimine: nam neq vxorem vnq habuit neq filios·septuaginta et quatuor annoꝛ obijt in bithinia·plen⁹ spiritu sancto. Qui cū iam scripta eſſent euāgelia· p̃ macheū quideₑ in iudea· p̃ marcū aūt in italia:sancto instigante spiritu in achaie partibₑ hoc scripsit euangeliū: significans etiā ipe in principio ante suū alia eſſe descripta. Cui extra ea q̄ ordo euāgelice dispoſitionis expoſcit ea maxime neceſſitas laboris fuit:ut primū grecis fidelibₑ omni p̃phetatione venturi in carne dei crhi manifeſtata humanitate ne iudaicis fabulis attenti: in solo legis deſiderio teneretur: vel ne hereticis fabulis et ſtultis solicitationibₑ ſeducti excideret a veritate elaboraret:dehinc·ut in principio euangelij iohānis natiuitate preſumpta·cui euangelium ſcriberet et in quo elect⁹ ſcriberet indicaret: cōteſtās i ſe cōpleta eſſe·q̄ eſſent ab alijs inchoata. Cui ideo poſt baptiſmū filij dei a p̃fectione generationis i cristo impleₑ repetenda a p̃ncipio natiuitatis humaₑ ne poteſtas p̃miſſa e̅: ut requirentibₑ demonſtraret in quo apprehendēs erat p̃ nathan filiū dauid introitu recurrentis i deū generationis admiſſo. indiſparabilis dı p̃dicās in homīibus criſtū ſuū·p̃fecti opus hois redire in ſe p̃ filiū facere: qui p̃ dauid patreₑ venientibus iter p̃bebat in cristo. Cui luce non immerito etiā ſcribedoꝛ actuū apoſtoloꝛ poteſtas i miniſterio datur:ut deo in deū pleno et filio p̃dictionis extincto·orationeₑ ab apoſtolis

facta·ſorte domini electionis numerₒ compleretur: itaq paulus cōſummatione apoſtolicis actibₑ daretꝰ·quē diu cōtra ſtimulū recalcitrantē dūs elegiſſet. Quod et legentibₑ aut requirentibₑ deū·et ſi p̃ ſingula expediri a nobis vtile fuerat:ſcientes tamē q̄ operātem agricolā oporteat de ſuis fructibus edere·vitauin⁹ publicā curioſitatem: ne nō tā volentibₑ deū demoſtrare videremur·quā faſtidientibus prodidiſſe. Explicit p̃facio Incipit euangelium ſecundū lucam : Prohemium ip̃ ſius beati luce in euangelium ſuum.

Quoniā quideₑ multi conati ſut ordinare narrationes q̄ i nobis complete ſut reꝛ·ſicut tradidereūt nobis q̄ ab initio ipſi viderūt· et miniſtri fuerūt ſermonis·viſu e̅ et michi aſſecuto omnia a p̃ncipio diligēter tibi ſcribere optie theophile : ut cognoſcas eoꝛ verboꝛ de q̄ibₑ eruditꝰ es veritateₑ. I.

Fuit in diebus herodis regis iudee ſacerdos quidam nomine zacharias de vice abia·et vxor illi de filiabus aaron : et nomen eius elizabeth. Erant autem iuſti ambo ante deum: incedentes in omnibus mandatis et iuſtificationibus domini ſine querella. Et non erat illis filius·eo q̄ eſſet elizabeth ſterilis:et ambo proceſſiſſent i diebz ſuis. Factū eſt aūt cū ſacerdotio fungeretur zacharias in ordine vicis ſue ante deū:ſcdm cōſuetudineₑ ſacerdotij ſorte exijt ut incenſum poneret ingreſſus in templū domini. Et oīs multitudo ip̃ſi erat orās foris hora incenſi. Apparuit autem illi angelus dñi:ſtans a dextris altaris

The only ancient writing material that fits this description is parchment. Like the attempts of most other rulers to destroy writings they did not like, King Jehojakim's destructive act was a failure. The words of Jeremiah have survived despite the king's evil deed.

*Parchment from Pergamon*

In the second century B.C., the king of Egypt waged war against Pergamon, a small kingdom in what is now the northwestern part of Turkey. While the war was in progress, the Egyptian king prohibited the export of papyrus to Pergamon, hoping that the lack of writing material would paralyze the machinery of government and force Pergamon to surrender. But, as history shows us, a nation with ingenuity can turn adversity to its advantage, and the people of Pergamon were no exception. Forced to find a new writing material, they turned to parchment and used it with great success. Eventually, the people of Pergamon built one of the greatest libraries of the ancient world, and the use of parchment was one of its specialties.

According to the Roman author Varro, parchment was actually invented in Pergamon, but this story is disputed by modern scholars, who

*Left:* A page from the first Latin Bible printed in Europe in 1456

point out that parchment was used for writing long before the second century B.C. But although parchment itself may not have originated in Pergamon, the word "parchment" apparently did. Pergamon became so well known for its fine quality parchment that the Romans began to call the material "pergamentum," which means "of Pergamon" in Latin. By the time the word found its way into the English language, it had become "parchment."

*Writing on Parchment*

Texts on both papyrus and parchment scrolls were written in columns from top to bottom, and they continued from one sheet to another. Sometimes there were two columns to a sheet, and sometimes only one. In either case, the ancient scribe marked out vertical lines that indicated the margins of each column. Then within these vertical margins, he measured the number of horizontal lines which he could allow for each column, leaving wide margins at the top and bottom. For parchment scrolls, these horizontal lines were scratched into the surface with a sharp pen knife; these faint lines can still be seen on some of the ancient scrolls. Writing in most languages was done on top of the lines,

A close-up of one section of the Dead Sea Scroll

as we write in English, but Hebrew was written underneath the line, as if the letters were clothes hanging on a clothesline. This is mainly because the Hebrew alphabet contains many deep descending letters, like the English lower case y and j.

As a writing material, parchment differs from papyrus in certain important respects. For one thing, it is more durable and can withstand harder use. Unlike papyrus scrolls, which had to be frequently recopied, parchment scrolls tended to last for a long time. One of the disadvantages of parchment, however (especially during the early centuries of its manufacture), was that the outer, or hair, side of the skin was a different color and texture from the inner, or flesh, side. The flesh side was naturally smoother, and originally only this side was used for writing — the hair side was left for the outside of the book or scroll.

## The First Books

At first, parchment was used mainly in scrolls, and the individual sheets were sewn together just as if

*Left:* One of the famous Dead Sea Scrolls, described in Chapter VI

they had been sheets of papyrus. To this day, in fact, the sacred Torah scrolls used in synagogues are made of fine parchment sheets sewn together to form rolls. But although scrolls are pleasing to look at and easy to read from beginning to end they have certain disadvantages. If you want to look things up in different parts of the scroll, you must unroll one part of the scroll — and roll up the other part — every time you turn to a different place. After a while this can become very tiring, and it creates a great deal of wear and tear on the scroll itself.

If the sheets of writing material are folded, however, they can be made into the pages of a book, which is far easier to use. The main difficulty that this presented with papyrus was that the soft and somewhat delicate material tended to tear or break where it was folded, especially after the folds had been opened and closed many times. Yet even when papyrus was still in general use, some ancient people began to use it this way instead of in long scrolls. The use of parchment, which almost never broke or tore, speeded this transition from scrolls to books.

The earliest books were made by folding the sheets of parchment or papyrus in the middle and placing them inside one another. Usually, 8 sheets were used, for a total of 16 pages. This arrangement is called a "quire." The sheets were stitched together at the place where they were folded. For a whole text several quires would be placed side by side in their proper order. Then the stitching at their backs was bound together to form a book. This basic method of making books is still used today for making hard-cover books, even though the parchment has been replaced by paper and the hand copying has been replaced by printing.

Until the invention of printing, every scroll and book in existence was an original manuscript: the word "manuscript" itself comes from the Latin *manu scriptum,* or "written by hand." The way in which the ancient manuscripts were prepared, however, is a fascinating story in itself.

*Left:* Moses reading a scroll

# IV   PREPARING MANUSCRIPTS

Before printing was invented, you could not go into the nearest bookshop and simply buy a copy of a book you needed. You either had to copy the entire book yourself or you had to pay someone else to copy it for you. The ancients used two different methods for copying. With one method, a scribe (a person who wrote or copied for a living) would sit with the original opened in front of him and copy what he read. In the other method, one person would read the manuscript aloud, and another person would write down what he heard. Certain wealthy Romans — who would probably be called "publishers" today — used slaves to do copying on a large scale. One of the slaves would sit and read a manuscript aloud while the others — sometimes as many as a hundred — would write. In this way, a hundred copies of a popular work (in our language, a "best-seller") could be produced at once.

*Left:* A scribe of the Middle Ages (repeated from color section)

## Errors in Copying

These two basic ways of copying manuscripts resulted in two different kinds of errors. If a manuscript was copied by eye, a careless scribe might jump from one place to the other and omit entire lines — or even paragraphs — at once. (This was particularly likely to happen if some important word occurred in two different places on the same page.) Or he might accidently repeat a whole passage, writing it twice. In other cases, certain letters which resembled each other might be confused, and a word misspelled as a result. Such an error might greatly alter the meaning of a text, especially in Greek and Latin. If a manuscript was copied by ear, there was always the possibility that two words which sounded alike might become confused, and that one would be written where the other was meant.

In ancient times, special correctors were employed who would try to correct as many of these mistakes as possible, but they still allowed many errors to remain. As time passed and a scroll was passed from one person to another, one of its owners might decide to correct a word or passage that he thought was incorrect. Sometimes the new owner simply crossed out what he believed was an error and wrote in the correction above it. Modern scholars greatly prefer this, since it gives them the opportunity to read both versions and to decide for themselves which one is more likely to be correct. In other cases, however, an owner would first remove the old writing by scraping or washing the ink away before

inserting his own version. While this method may not look as messy as the first, the original writing is lost forever, and scholars can only guess at what the manuscript once said.

Correcting the errors and faults in a manuscript is called "emending," and the task of emending ancient manuscripts has become a special science, requiring special skills and training. People who do this important and difficult work must not only be able to read the ancient writing itself, but they must also be familiar with all the different versions of the particular text they are studying. As you can imagine, there have been many lengthy and complicated argu-

*Above:* One of the Dead Sea Scrolls showing corrections that were made in the text

*Right:* A close-up of the Dead Sea Scroll

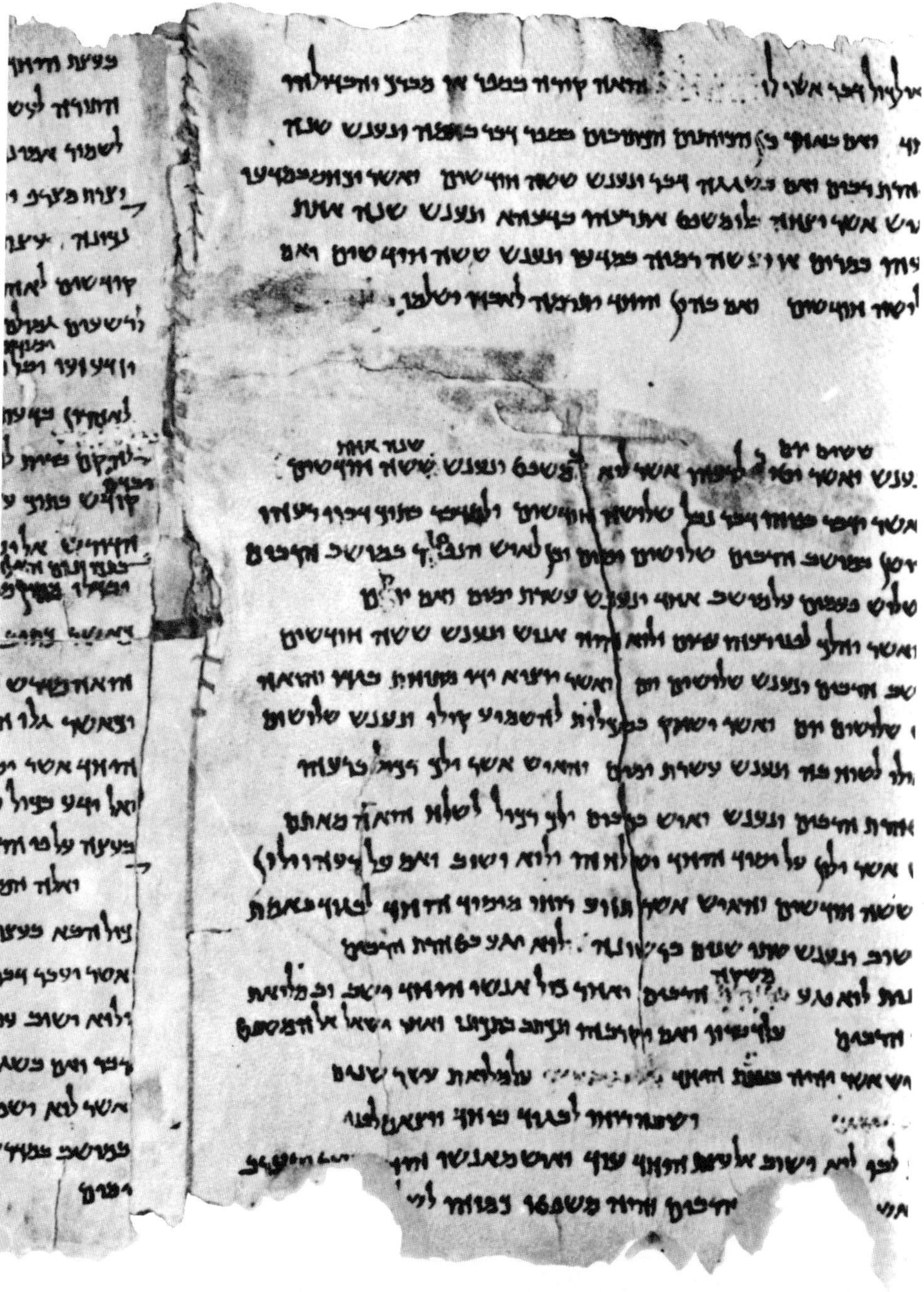

ments among these scientists concerning the precise meaning of certain passages in ancient texts. One scholar, perhaps because he was angry that other scholars disagreed with him, actually spilled ink over a sentence that he and his colleagues were arguing about. This made it impossible for anyone to examine the original version and perhaps prove him wrong. Of course, he claimed it was an accident, but it is doubtful that many people believed him.

## Copying the Hebrew Bible

The Hebrew Bible — which Christians usually call the "Old Testament," — was written during the first millennium B.C., but the final decision about exactly which holy writings should be included in it was not made until the second century A.D. The biblical manuscript presented certain problems to the Hebrews who studied them, however, because they seemed to contain a large number of errors. Yet the Hebrews were reluctant to tamper with their sacred texts. In the seventh century A.D., a group of Hebrew scholars called "Massoretes," or "Men of Tradition," began the work of establishing a correct text of the Bible. As their work proceeded, they discovered that the original manuscripts contained almost 1,500 verses with possible errors. The Massoretes dared not change the sacred writings themselves, so instead they noted on the margin what they believed to have been the correct word. In this way, they created the difference between what is called in Hebrew the *qeri* (the correct way) and the *ketib* (what was originally written).

The Hebrews prepared copies of the Bible manuscripts according to a very complicated set of instructions, which had to be followed carefully and exactly. This was especially important in making copies of the Torah scrolls used in synagogues. (These scrolls contain the first five books of the Bible.) The instructions themselves were framed like pictures. They described exactly which materials should be used for making the scrolls, how the sheets of parchment should be fastened together, how to make the proper kind of ink, how to mark the lines on the parchment before a single word is written, how many columns of writing could be put on each scroll, and even such things as the correct number of letters for each line of text!

Before the Hebrew scribe could begin the work of copying a text of the Bible, he had to take a ritual bath, so as to purify himself. No

*Right:* Part of a Torah scroll copied by one of the Massoretes

**עמוד ימני (יהושע א)**

ויהי אחרי מות משה עבד ״
יהוה ויאמר יהוה אל יהושע
בן נון משרת משה לאמר ׃
משה עבדי מת ועתה קום עבר
את הירדן הזה אתה וכל העם
הזה אל הארץ אשר אנכי נתן
להם לבני ישראל כל מקום
אשר תדרך כף רגלכם בו לכם
נתתיו כאשר דברתי אל משה
מהמדבר והלבנון הזה ועד
הנהר הגדול נהר פרת כל ארץ
החתים ועד הים הגדול מבוא
השמש יהיה גבולכם לא
יתיצב איש לפניך כל ימי חייך
כאשר הייתי עם משה אהיה
עמך לא ארפך ולא אעזבך
חזק ואמץ כי אתה תנחיל את
העם הזה את הארץ אשר
נשבעתי לאבותם לתת להם
רק חזק ואמץ מאד לשמר
לעשות ככל התורה אשר
צוך משה עבדי אל תסור
ממנו ימין ושמאל למען
תשכיל בכל אשר תלך
לא ימוש ספר התורה הזה מפיך
והגית בו יומם ולילה למען
תשמר לעשות ככל הכתוב
בו כי אז תצליח את דרכך ואז

**עמוד אמצעי (יהושע א)**

תשכיל הלא צויתיך חזק
ואמץ אל תערץ ואל תחת
עקב ׳ יהוה אלהיך בכל אשר
תלך ׃
ויצו יהושע את שטרי העם
לאמר עברו בקרב המחנה
וצוו את העם לאמר הכינו
לכם צדה כי בעוד שלשת
ימים אתם עברים את הירדן
הזה לבוא לרשת את הארץ
אשר יהוה אלהיכם נתן לכם
לרשתה ׃
ולראובני ולגדי ולחצי שבט
המנשה אמר יהושע לאמר ׃
זכור את הדבר אשר צוה אתכם
משה עבד יהוה לאמר ׳
יהוה אלהיכם מניח לכם
ונתן לכם את הארץ הזאת
נשיכם טפכם ומקניכם ישבו
בארץ אשר נתן לכם משה
בעבר הירדן ואתם תעברו
חמשים לפני אחיכם כל
גבורי החיל ועזרתם אותם ׃
עד אשר יניח יהוה לאחיכם
ככם וירשו גם המה את
הארץ אשר יהוה אלהיכם
נתן להם ושבתם לארץ
ירשתכם וירשתם אותה ׳

**עמוד שמאלי (יהושע א–ב)**

אשר נתן לכם משה עבד
יהוה בעבר הירדן מזרח
השמש ויענו את יהושע
לאמר כל אשר צויתנו נעשה
ואל כל אשר תשלחנו נלך
ככל אשר שמענו אל משה
כן נשמע אליך רק יהיה יהוה
אלהיך עמך כאשר היה
עם משה כל איש אשר ימרה
את פיך ולא ישמע את
דבריך לכל אשר תצונו
יומת רק חזק ואמץ ׃

וישלח יהושע בן נון מן
השטים שנים אנשים מרגלים
חרש לאמר לכו ראו את
הארץ ואת יריחו וילכו
ויבאו בית אשה זונה ושמה
רחב וישכבו שמה ׃ ויאמר
למלך יריחו לאמר הנה
אנשים באו הנה הלילה
מבני ישראל לחפר את
הארץ ׃ וישלח מלך יריחו
אל רחב לאמר הוציאי
האנשים הבאים אליך אשר
באו לביתך כי לחפר את כל
הארץ באו ׃ ותקח האשה
את שני האנשים ותצפנו ׳

אֵלֶּה פְקוּדֵי בְּנֵי יִשְׂרָאֵל
לְבֵית אֲבֹתָם כָּל פְּקוּדֵי
הַמַּחֲנֹת לְצִבְאֹתָם שֵׁשׁ
מֵאוֹת אֶלֶף וּשְׁלֹשֶׁת
אֲלָפִים וַחֲמֵשׁ מֵאוֹת
וַחֲמִשִּׁים וְהַלְוִיִּם לֹא
הָתְפָּקְדוּ בְּתוֹךְ בְּנֵי
יִשְׂרָאֵל כַּאֲשֶׁר צִוָּה
יְהוָה אֶת מֹשֶׁה וַיַּעֲשׂוּ
בְּנֵי יִשְׂרָאֵל כְּכֹל אֲשֶׁר
צִוָּה יְהוָה אֶת מֹשֶׁה
כֵּן חָנוּ לְדִגְלֵיהֶם וְכֵן
נָסָעוּ אִישׁ לְמִשְׁפְּחֹתָיו
עַל בֵּית אֲבֹתָיו׃

matter how well he knew the passages he was about to copy, he was forbidden to write the text from memory. Instead, he was required to sit with another scroll open before him and refer to it for each word that he wrote. He was required to take special care of his pen and ink, and he was forbidden to write the four-letter name of God with a pen freshly dipped in ink, lest he make a blot. The space between each word had to be the width of a narrow consonant, and the space between each consonant had to be the width of a human hair! While he was writing, the scribe was required to rid his mind of all distracting thoughts and concentrate on the task before him. In fact, it is written that "even if he were spoken to by a king, he should not answer." These special rules, first set forth many centuries ago, are followed by devout Hebrew scribes to this day.

Such strict rules applied mainly to the copying of sacred texts, and they were not normally followed for literary or political writings. The ancient Greeks, however, treated the texts of Homer in more or less the same way as the Jews treated their Bible. The number of lines in each book of the *Odyssey* and the *Iliad* were carefully counted, and — since the Greeks did not dare change the original text — special signs were invented to mark lines that were considered incorrect.

## Copying by the Monks of Europe

Perhaps the most elaborate system for preparing manuscripts was practiced during the Middle Ages in the monasteries of the Catholic Church. The monks of this period — especially the Benedictine monks — regarded copying as important and praiseworthy work, as pleasing to God as tilling the soil, and almost as important as praying. The monks therefore spent their waking hours praying, working in the fields, and copying manuscripts. The work of copying was done in a special writing room called a "scriptorium," where the monk sat with a copy of the original placed before him.

As more and more copies of manuscripts were needed, the monks of Europe began to find good parchment more and more difficult to obtain. Therefore the monks were often tempted to erase an old text, which they could easily do with a sponge, and write a new text on the fine old parchment that remained. Thus the many books which the monks needed, such as prayer books, books of psalms, and learned works

*Left:* Close-up of the script used by the Massoretes

on religious subjects, came often to be written in bold, black script over the faded lines of an ancient author. Such manuscripts are called "palimpsests." To us, of course, the ancient text is more valuable than the newer writings, and fortunately a way has been found to read the original lines of the palimpsest. When the palimpsest is placed under certain kinds of light produced by modern scientific apparatus, the old writing suddenly becomes clearly visible again, as if by magic. In this way, the works of several ancient authors, lawyers, and teachers have been recovered. Once in a while, a palimpsest contains a text that has been covered up by a copy of a still more ancient work. For example, there is a translation of Homer's *Iliad* written over a text of the Christian apostle St. Paul.

The importance of manuscripts to the monks of the Middle Ages can also be seen in the care with which they kept their books safe from harm or loss. The manuscripts were kept in a library and were cared for by a librarian. The man in charge of the monastery was called an "abbot," and many of these abbots were eager to borrow manuscripts so that they might copy them for their own collections. The Abbot of Ferrières in France, for example, was known to be always ready to borrow manuscripts from others but very careful about lending any of his own, fearing that they might be lost.

In the libraries of these monasteries, deep silence was the rule. In some cases a special sign language was invented so that a borrower could tell the librarian what books he wanted without having to speak at all. If, for example, he wanted a book of psalms, he would hold his hands over his head to represent the crown of David, the king of the ancient Hebrews known as the royal psalmist. On the other hand, if the borrower wanted a manuscript by an author who was not approved by the Church — such as an early pagan writer — he made a sign that looked like a dog scratching himself behind the ear. This was to show that the work he wanted was regarded with contempt.

## Illuminated Manuscripts

The religious manuscripts that the monks prepared in the Middle Ages are especially famous for their brilliant and beautiful illustrations. The art of illustrating a manuscript is called "illumination," and the story of illuminated manuscripts goes back thousands of years before the Middle Ages, to the time of the

*Right:* A palimpsest showing Latin writing on top of an ancient text

Egyptian hieroglyphs

ancient Egyptians. In fact, the idea that pictures possess a sacred or magical power really goes back to the time of the cave men, who often drew pictures and signs on the walls of their caves in the practice of their own religious rituals.

The ancient Egyptians wrote with symbols called "hieroglyphs," which were simplified pictures that sometimes represented the object in the picture but more often represented a sound, just like the letters of the alphabet. Aside from the hieroglyphics themselves, the Egyptians made numerous images and symbols of the gods, and these drawings were thought to possess magical power. One of the oldest of all illuminated manuscripts is the Egyptian *Book of the Dead,* a kind of guide to the afterlife. A copy of this book was

*Right:* An illustration from an Egyptian Book of the Dead, showing the weighing of the soul.

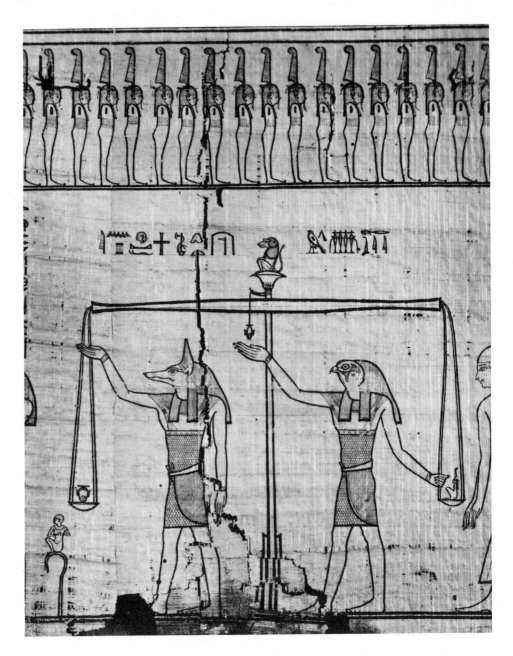

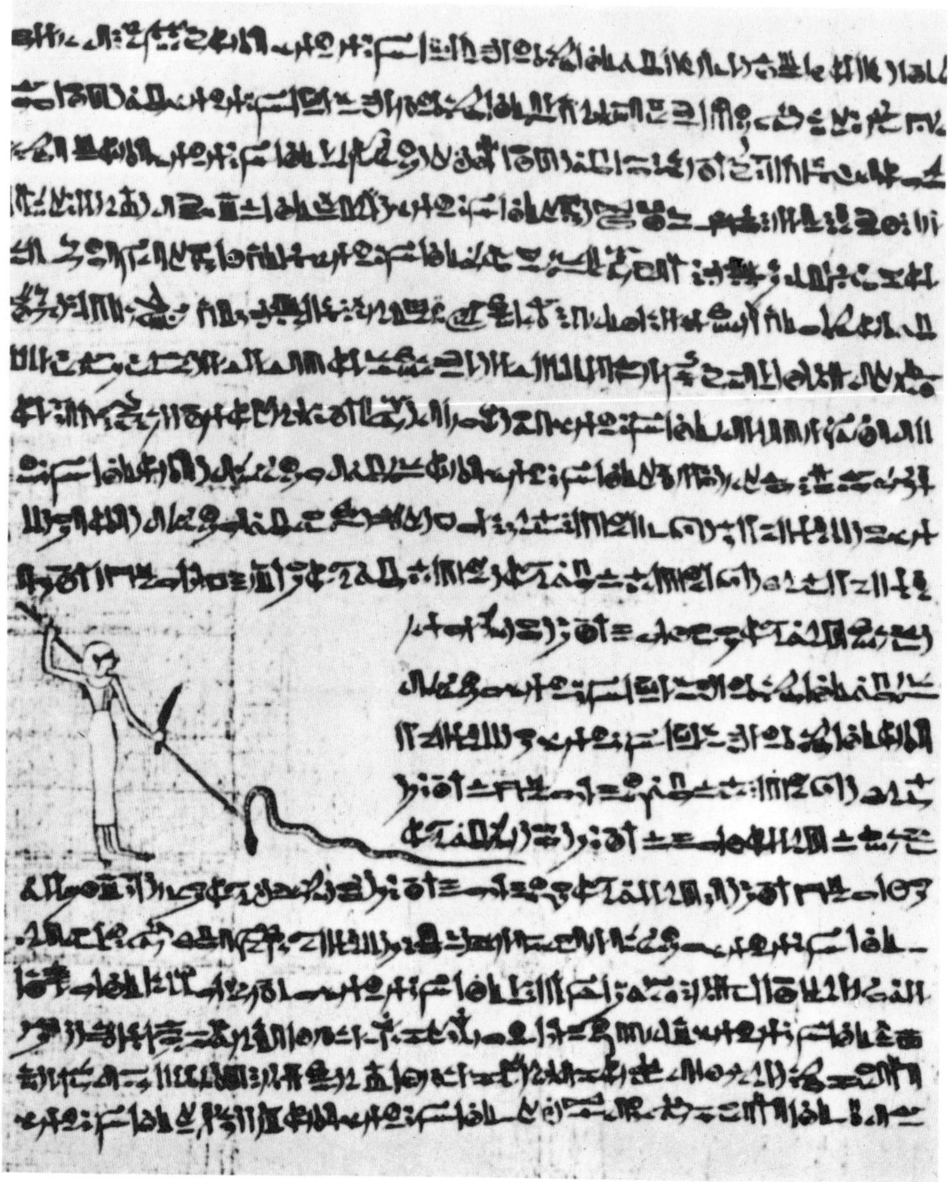

An Egyptian Book of the Dead

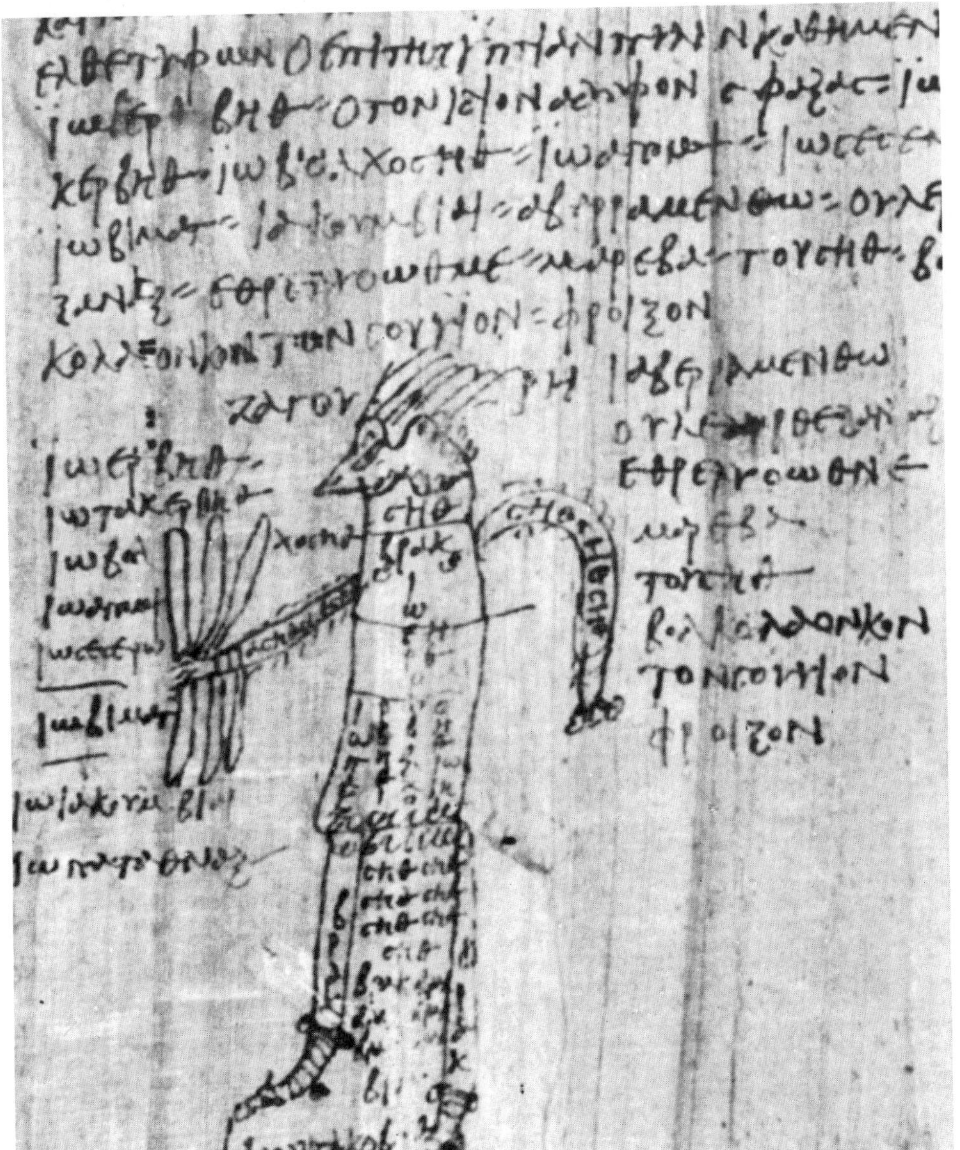

A Greek magical papyrus

*Above and below:* Egyptian satirical illustrations on papyrus

placed in the tombs of rich commoners so that, after death, the deceased could give the correct answers to the judges of his soul, who would examine his deeds. It was also intended to help him find his way in the "nether world" — a place the Egyptians believed existed beneath the surface of the earth, to which the soul was believed to go after death. For each action in the Book of the Dead, there is a separate picture, in which the main characters appear again and again. Perhaps from this example ancient people learned to divide a story into a number of single acts, with a picture for each act.

The ancient Greeks probably became familiar with illuminated manuscripts during the last 300 years before Christ, when they ruled Egypt. But before this time the sculpture on Greek buildings shows the same characteristic of depicting a single important character in a number of different scenes, performing a number of different actions.

Other Greek manuscripts on scientific subjects are illuminated with what must be some of the earliest technical illustrations in recorded history. A Greek doctor named Dioscorides, for example, wrote manuals on botany and zoology, and his manuscripts were illuminated with pictures of the plants and animals he described. Other Greek authors illuminated their texts on medical subjects, thus adding greatly to the value and usefulness of their writings.

No one really knows when the first illuminated manuscript of Homer's writings was made. The oldest surviving illuminated Greek manuscript dates from the fourth century A.D.

Detail of the Egyptian illustration showing a lion and a unicorn playing checkers

An Egyptian illuminated manuscript showing a sacrifice

Illustrations for the Bible were probably inspired by these early Greek illuminations, and some of the biblical stories — such as that of Adam, Eve, and the serpent — may have even been influenced by the desire to make them more suitable for illustration.

The oldest illuminated manuscript of the Bible which has survived is a copy of the story of Genesis from the sixth century A.D. This and other surviving illuminated texts, however, are (with one exception) not scrolls but codices. These are manuscripts that are folded flat rather than being rolled up. Since codices were developed after rolled scrolls, and since scrolls were easier to illuminate, it is almost certain that older illuminated scrolls once existed.

The beautiful illuminated manuscripts that told religious stories were not really illuminated Bibles. In the time of the ancient Greeks and Romans, illuminated manuscripts contained a written text that told a biblical story. But the story was not an actual quotation from the Bible itself. The Jews who spoke Greek (and translated the Hebrew Scriptures into Greek) considered the Bible itself too holy to be decorated by pictures. And in the original Hebrew version of the Bible, all illustrations were absolutely forbidden. Later on, Christians did illuminate actual texts

*Right:* A text in Latin, showing some of the signs of the Zodiac

quae notata est & stellis
xxx. exquibus duae claræ
castere obscurae sunt..

Capricornus habet & stellas
in singulis cornibus singulas
in naso claeram .i. in capite .ii.
sub collo .i. in pectore .ii.
in pede priori .i. in summi
tectae pedis .i. in dorso .vii.
in uentre .v. in cauda .ii.
claerar summa xxiiii.

Sagittarius habet & stellas
in capite .ii. in acumine

sagittae .ii. in dextro cubito
.i. in manu .i. in uentre .i.
claeram uidorsi .iii.
in cauda .i. in genu priori
.i. in summo pede .i.
in posteriori. gestiri
fiunt. xiii.

Aquilae habet & stellas .iiii.
& his media claera est
sagitta habet & stellas .iiii.
in summo .i. in medio .i.
in alia summitectae
.ii.

Delphinus habet & stellas
in ore .i. in cornu .ii. in
uentris pinnulis .iii.
in dorso .i. in cauda .ii.
omnes .viiii.

A page from a Byzantine Bible showing Moses receiving the Ten Commandments from the hand of God

A page from an illuminated New Testament showing Jesus entering Jerusalem

A papyrus fragment with an illustration of the ancient Greek poet Homer

from the Bible that were written in Latin or Greek. In one respect, however, the Hebrews' ancient reluctance to illuminate the Bible itself had its effect until the 11th century A.D. Until this time, even in the most detailed of the illuminated Christian manuscripts, God was never represented as a whole person. Rather, as it had been done in the frescoes and mosaics of the ancient Jewish synagogues, the power of God was represented by nothing more than a single, outstretched hand.

# V THE SURVIVAL OF ANCIENT LITERATURE

Almost all of the ancient literature which has survived did so because it was preserved on parchment, even though much of it was originally written on papyrus and scrolls. But as long as every book and scroll in existence had to be copied by hand, there was the danger that only one copy of some texts would be in existence. If that one copy were to be destroyed, the work would be lost forever.

Thus perhaps the greatest achievement of the copyists of the Middle Ages was that they preserved the writings of ancient authors until the development of printing. Now that most ancient writings have been printed in thousands or even millions of copies, there is little danger that any more of them will be lost. Unfortunately, however, the monks did not copy all of the ancient literature which still existed during their time. Instead, they selected the works which they considered most interesting and most important. In the end, only about ten per cent of ancient Greek literature — and only about one-third of the Latin literature from Roman times — was preserved. Although we deeply regret what has been lost of ancient Latin and Greek literature, we are truly grateful to the devoted scribes of the Middle Ages who preserved what we do have. If it had not been for their efforts, we might know little of the great writings of history, drama, poetry, science, medicine, politics, and philosophy of the ancient Greek and Roman civilizations.

## Greek and Latin Literature

There were some important differences between the way Greek literature was preserved and the way Latin literature was preserved, and these differences account for the fact that so much of the Greek literature was lost. Very few of the European monks could read Greek, but most of them could read Latin. Thus the Latin writings were read, understood, and copied, while the Greek writings were often ignored and lost. In fact, when the monks copied a work that contained passages in Greek, they would often fail to copy the Greek passages at all. Instead, they would write, "These words are in Greek and cannot be read."

At this time, Greek literature was still flourishing in the Byzantine Empire, which included Greece, Turkey, and other nearby lands. The Byzantines themselves spoke Greek, and they were constantly copying and recopying the ancient texts which they possessed. Unfortunately, they did not continue to use all the Greek manuscripts that they originally had. They used the writings of the ancient Greeks mainly in schools, and of the many works which the Greeks produced the Byzantines chose only those which they felt would serve as the best models for instruction. All of the other works tended to be ignored. They were seldom read, and they were hardly ever recopied. In time, the manuscripts containing these other works were lost. Thus, of the 90 plays written by the brilliant Greek playwright Aristophanes, only 11 have survived, and these only because they were used in the Byzantine schools.

In the ninth century A.D., the Byzantines began a practice which further reduced the number of ancient texts that were to survive. Partly because they wanted to make it easier for people to look things up in their enormous libraries, they began to prepare digests and encyclopedias on various subjects. To do this, they would copy the most important passages from the writings on one particular subject — such as military strategy — and put it all together into a single volume. Various Byzantine rulers ordered their scribes to prepare encyclopedias on such subjects as history, language, agriculture, and medicine. In doing so, they took information from hundreds of original manuscripts. Once these

*Right above:* An illustrated manuscript of Homer's masterpiece, the *Iliad.* In this illustration, the goddess Aphrodite is pictured showing her hand to Zeus

*Right below:* This illustration from the *Iliad* shows the Greeks dragging their boats to the sea in preparation for the voyage home

*Overleaf left:* A battle scene from the *Iliad*

*Overleaf right:* Another battle scene from the *Iliad*

וידבר אל וֹחבקוק לכתוב את הבאות על    אל

על הדור האחרון ואת גמר הקץ לוא הודיעו

ואשר אמר למען ירוץ הקורא בו    רבמ

פשרו על מורה הצדק אשר הודיעו אל את    X

כול רזי דברי עבדיו הנבאים כיא עוד חזון

למועד יפח לקץ ולוא יכזב    ת

פשרו אשר יארוך הקץ האחרון ויתר על כול

אשר דברו הנבאים כיא רזי אל להפלא    נבור

אם יתמהמה חכה לו כיא בוא יבוא ולוא

יאחר    פשרו על אנשי האמת

עשי התורה אשר לוא ירפו ידיהם מעבודת    ב

האמת בהמשך עליהם הקץ האחרון כיא    יו

כול קצי אל יבואו לתכונם כאשר חקק    X

להמה ברזי ערמתו הנה עופלה לוא ישרה    ורבר

נפשו בו וצדיק באמונתו יחיה    ...

בשרו אשר וכפל עליהם

---

X    משאו על כול עושי התורה בצית יהודה אשר    נועיבבשם

יצילם אל מבית המשפט בעבור עמלם    רשען עשו ב

ואמנתם במורה הצדק ואף כיא הוני ולוא    אשר טו אתה

יפח אשר הרחיב כשאול נפשו וכא כמות לוא ישבעו    ותרשעם

ויאספו אליו כול הגוים ויקבצו אלו כול העמים    האחירונם ל

הלוא כולם משל עליו ישאו ומליצת חידות לו    ולא החוזב ה

ויאמרו הוי המרבה ולוא לו עד מתי ויכבד עליו    חול המטואל

עבטט    פשרו על הכוהן הרשע אשר    שרש אזק ו

נקרא על שם האמת בתחלת עומדו ובשר יכאשר משל    משיר על ח

בישראל רם לבו ויעזוב את אל ויבגוד בחוקים בעבור    חטיקן ואנשי

הון ויגזול ויקבוץ הון אנשי חמס אשר מרדו באל    נגמ לבלה

והון עמים לקח לוסיף עליו עוון אשמה ודרכי    על בחורי

תועבות פעל בכול נדת טמאה כיא בשעו ויקומו    כאחת קץ

עליו יקוצו בשועיו כבבה וחונח לגמאות למו    לתונם קעו

כי אתה שלותה גוים רבים וישלוכה כול יתר עמים    אחז ר

מדמי אדם וחמס ארץ קריה וכול יושבי בה    ...

encyclopedias and digests had been completed, however, the Byzantines found them so convenient to use that they rarely bothered to look things up in the original manuscripts any more. As time passed, these originals were gradually forgotten. No more copies of them were made, and eventually most of them were lost.

Of all the ancient authors, the Latin poet Virgil was one of the most popular. He was widely regarded as a prophet, and many people believed that he had predicted the coming of Christ. (Actually, the poem used to support this theory described, not Christ, but a young relative of the Roman Emperor Augustus.) Some people even considered Virgil a sorcerer, and his writings were used to predict the future. A person who wanted to know about his future would open the manuscript of Virgil and stick a needle into one of Virgil's poems. He would push the needle through the pages of the manuscript to see what had been written at the spot where the needle had stopped. This spot was supposed to contain the prophecy. This practice explains why many ancient manuscripts of Virgil are full of pin holes.

## The Greek Anthology

One happy exception to this gloomy story concerns a remarkable manuscript called the "Greek Anthology." An anthology is a collection of writings by different authors. In ancient times the Greeks applied this name to collections of poetry. (In Greek, the word itself means "garland of flowers.") One of the earliest of these collections was made by a Greek named Meleager, during the first century B.C. As later writers copied his anthology, they added other poems to the original collection, so that Meleager's anthology grew. At the same time, other writers made still other collections of Greek poetry, until after a few centuries there were a number of anthologies in existence. Finally, in A.D. 970, a Byzantine named Constantius Cephalas copied Meleager's anthology and a number of later ones into one great series of manuscripts, containing more than 6,000 poems by 320 different authors!

This great work was recopied in later years, and one of the copies, made in the 11th century A.D., eventually found its way to Germany, where it came into the possession of a German prince in the 16th century. (Because this prince held the title of Palatine Elector, the anthology also came to be known as the "Palatine Anthology.") After it had

been in Germany for many years, the Anthology was captured by the army of the Catholic League, whereupon it was taken to Rome and presented to the Vatican Library. After it had been in Rome for over 150 years, the Emperor Napoleon had it brought to Paris. When Napoleon's army was defeated a few years later, however, the Anthology was returned to Germany.

The story of the Greek Anthology is important not only because it shows how a priceless manuscript can survive through frequent travels and even through wars, but also because it is one case where gathering many different writings into a single work has helped to preserve much that might have otherwise been lost. The manuscript found in Germany by the Catholic League was the sole surviving copy of this magnificent collection. If that one copy had been lost, the greatest existing collection of ancient Greek poetry would have been lost with it.

Other precious manuscripts from ancient times were not as lucky as the Greek Anthology. When French crusaders captured the Greek city of Salonika in 1185, they found great quantities of manuscripts, which they sold by the shipload to Italian traders. The traders then sold the manuscripts to buyers from all over Europe. Some of the manuscripts were kept safe in homes, libraries, and museums, but many were lost. Some, in fact, were deliberately burned by people who thought that they contained ideas that went against the teachings of the Catholic Church.

Many ancient manuscripts never even reached Europe. When the crusaders captured the Byzantine capital city of Constantinople in the 13th century, they burned about 120,000 manuscripts. We can only guess at the number and variety of ancient manuscripts which have been lost or destroyed during the last 3,000 years. Eventually, some of the lost manuscripts will turn up somewhere, perhaps containing an ancient text that we have never seen or heard of before. But most of them are gone, never to be seen again.

## Jewish Literature

According to Jewish law, no writing in Hebrew letters could be thrown away, because it might contain the sacred name of God. Even manuscripts that had spoiled with age were kept in special storerooms in the Jewish synagogues. The most famous of these storerooms existed

*Left:* This Byzantine illuminated manuscript shows the evangelist St. Matthew preparing to write on a scroll

The oldest copy of the Ten Commandments in existence

in Cairo, Egypt, and great numbers of manuscripts, documents, and letters were found there by modern scholars, who brought them to England and America to study them at length. One of these manuscripts turned out to be an ancient Hebrew text that had previously been considered lost, dating from the second century B.C.

During the Greek and early Roman civilizations, a number of Jewish writers developed a large literature in the Greek language, which was used by most of the educated people of the ancient world at that time. But the Jews came into increasing conflict with Rome as time went on. Eventually the Romans crushed the Jewish rebellions and destroyed Jerusalem, the Jews' most important city and the site of their most sacred temple. After this, most Jews wanted to have little to do with the classical Greek and Roman cultures. Some of the writings of the Greek-speaking Jews were given the name "Books of the Heretics," because they contained opinions that most Jews did not agree with. These works eventually were forbidden for Jews to read and were marked for destruction. Because of this, most of these writings were lost.

Aside from the sacred biblical writings themselves, the only ancient Jewish writers whose works survived were those who had some connection with Christianity. Among these writers are the philosopher Philo and the soldier and historian Josephus. Josephus' descriptions of the destruction of Jerusalem and the temple seemed to agree with the prophecies of Jesus, and the Christians therefore preserved his works. The writings about the Maccabees, a Jewish family that ruled in Jerusalem during the first and second centuries B.C., was preserved because it was joined to the Greek translation of the Bible. For these reasons, much of our knowledge about the Jews' struggles with Rome — as well as the history of the sacred temple which the Romans destroyed — is due to the work of the early Christians.

## The Bible

The manuscripts of the Hebrew Bible were copied according to the strict rules of the Massoretes and carefully preserved. Even small scraps of biblical text were kept safe, including a papyrus manuscript from the second century B.C., which contains the oldest copy of the Ten Commandments in existence. Until the discovery of the Dead Sea Scrolls (which is the subject of the next chapter) this was the oldest manuscript of the Bible known to exist.

The oldest complete copies of the Hebrew Bible were made by the Massoretes during the 10th century A.D. A number of these manuscripts, which are written on parchment scrolls, have survived from that period, including the famous

*Keter-ha-Torah,* or "Crown of the Torah." The *Keter-ha-Torah,* a very beautiful copy of the Hebrew Bible, was written around the year A.D. 900, and it was kept in a synagogue in Aleppo, Syria, for centuries. When a riot broke out in the city of Aleppo, however, the synagogue was set on fire by an angry mob, and it burned to the ground. Scholars all over the world mourned the loss of this priceless Torah scroll. A small group of people knew, however, that the *Keter ha-Torah* had been secretly rescued from the flames and would be taken to Israel. It is now in the holy city of Jerusalem, where it is kept under careful guard.

The Christian churches did not use the Hebrew Bible itself. Instead, they used a Greek translation of it made by Jews who knew both Hebrew and Greek. This version of the Bible was first made more than a century before the birth of Christ, but the oldest complete manuscript of it that remains was made in the fourth century A.D. This manuscript is a codex of the finest parchment (called "vellum"), and it is called the "Codex Sinaiticus."

## The Codex Sinaiticus

In the year 1844, a biblical scholar named Tischendorf visited the ancient monastery of St. Catherine on the slopes of Mount Sinai, in Sinai peninsula. While he was at the monastery, Tischendorf noticed that the monks had collected the loose pages of a vellum manuscript in a basket, to use for fuel. On the pages of the manuscript, Tischendorf recognized the beautiful Greek script of the fourth century A.D. You can imagine how he felt when he learned that this was the next batch to be burned in the oven! Tischendorf begged the monks to allow him to take some of the manuscript back to Germany to present to his king. The monks decided to keep the manuscript, but they gave Tischendorf 43 pages to take back with him. Fifteen years later, he returned to the monastery of St. Catherine again, and this time he persuaded the monks to give him the rest of the manuscript, which he presented to the Russian emperor. The ancient manuscript came to be known as the "Codex Sinaiticus," and it remained in Russia until 1933. In that year, the British Museum bought the Codex for 100,000 English pounds — over a quarter of a million dollars.

The Codex Sinaiticus is hundreds of years older than the *Keter-*

ha-Torah, and it is the oldest copy of the Christian Bible in existence. It is incredible to think that this priceless manuscript was once nearly burned as cooking fuel.

## The Talmud

The Jews possess another group of important writings in addition to the Bible. These are the traditional teachings and laws of the Jewish people, together with the commentaries of the many Jewish scholars who have studied them over the centuries. For a long time, the laws of the Jewish people could only be memorized, for it was forbidden to write them down. In the second century A.D., however, after the Jewish nation had been crushed by the Roman Empire, these laws and teachings were put in writing. From that time on, the Talmud was diligently studied by Jewish scholars, and manuscripts of its various sections were carefully copied.

In fact, the Jews have had a strong tradition of writing and scholarship ever since ancient times. For centuries, almost every Jewish boy has been taught to read and write, and the Jews have produced a great number of manuscripts over the last 2,000 years. During the Middle Ages, however, the Jews were often persecuted, and many of their manuscripts were lost or destroyed. Thus, although the Jews did make new copies of the Talmud, almost all of the original manuscripts were lost. When printing was invented in the 15th century, many copies of the Talmud were printed, and there was no longer any real danger that the Talmud itself would ever be lost. But the old manuscripts continued to disappear, and only five or six complete copies have survived.

Even the most complete Jewish manuscripts often do not contain everything they are supposed to, because Christian censors sometimes crossed out or removed passages in the Hebrew texts that they felt were offensive to the teachings of Christianity. However, the Jews were sometimes able to note down the forbidden passages before they were destroyed, and in some cases the lost passages have been restored by means of these old notes. Strangely enough, some Jewish writings were actually preserved by those who took the Jews' manuscripts away from them. A number of these manuscripts were given to the Catholic Church, where they often found their way into religious libraries, where they were relatively safe, and scholars could study them at their leisure.

## The Search for Ancient Literature

Almost 1,500 years have passed since the ancient world came to an end with the collapse of the Roman Empire. We have seen how certain people — especially the Christian monks, the Hebrew scholars, and the Byzantine teachers and librarians — devoted much effort to studying and preserving the literature that the ancients produced. We also know that they only preserved certain ancient works which happened to interest them, such as religious works and the literature used in schools. It was not until the end of the Middle Ages that people began to realize that *any* ancient manuscript might be of enormous value to mankind as a whole.

The Middle Ages came to an end in the 15th century A.D. By that time, the people of Europe had begun to take a new interest in the literary, artistic, and scientific work which the ancients had begun so brilliantly, but which had been largely neglected in Europe for a thousand years. This new birth of interest in intellectual pursuits — called the "Renaissance" (a French word meaning "rebirth") — first began in Italy. For this reason, Italian writers and scholars were the first Europeans to develop the passionate interest in ancient writing which all of Europe soon came to share, and which we have continued to feel to the present day.

The Italian poet Petrarch spent his entire life searching for ancient manuscripts. In 1333, he found two previously unknown speeches of the great Roman statesman and philosopher Cicero. Petrarch was thrilled at this discovery, especially since Cicero's speeches are considered to be the most beautiful speeches ever written in the Latin language. But Petrarch's good fortune was not over. Twelve years later, he had the supreme happiness of finding a copy of Cicero's letters, one of the richest sources of information about Roman life ever found. Petrarch copied the whole manuscript himself, and he even wrote a letter to Cicero's ghost, to tell him that the letters had been found. Although Petrarch loved all of ancient literature, he never learned Greek. When he was 51, he was given a manuscript of Homer in the original Greek, but he was never able to read it.

Another Italian writer named Bocaccio was a friend of Petrarch, and he shared Petrarch's love of ancient manuscripts. Bocaccio learned to read Greek, and — in his search for new manuscripts — he visited many of the libraries that the monks of the Middle Ages had established in their monasteries. By the 14th century, these splendid old libraries had become sadly neglected, however, and the monks of that time no longer seemed to appreciate the value of the manuscripts that were in their care. Bocaccio told how he visited the monastery of Monte Cassino, just to see the famous library there. The monks pointed the way and said, "Go up if you like, but nobody ever goes there any more." In a large room full of books and dust, Bocaccio found manuscripts with many pages missing. The ignorant monks had been tearing out pages by the handful, to make into psalm books that they sold for a few pennies a copy. The monks were also tearing off strips from the margins of old manuscripts and selling them as magic charms to ward off evil. In this library, Bocaccio found works by the great Roman historian Tacitus. These are now safely stored in a library in Florence, Italy, where Bocaccio and Petrarch both lived and worked.

In the years that followed, the spirit of the Renaissance spread throughout Europe. When the Byzantine capital of Constantinople was taken by the Turks in 1453, many learned Byzantines fled to the West. These refugees brought with them not only their thorough knowledge of Greek but also many important manuscripts of ancient Greek writings, further enriching the libraries and universities of Europe. In the centuries that have passed since the beginning of the Renaissance, many other scholars have searched for manuscripts of the lost ancient writings. Of course, as the few that survive are found and collected, new discoveries become even more difficult to make. Yet as recently as 1902, a new manuscript of a work by Tacitus was found in a private library in Italy. Today scholars continue to hope for future discoveries.

The problem of the survival of ancient literature was changed forever by the invention of printing in the 15th century. When thousands of copies of a work exist, the chances are extremely small that *all* of them will ever be lost or destroyed. At first, printed books were not always accepted by the educated people of Renaissance Europe. When a certain wealthy and important Italian family wanted to establish a private library, for example, they hired Vespasiano Da Portici, an important bookseller. Da Portici engaged the services of 54 copyists, who spent two years producing 200 books by hand. Da Portici was also hired by an Italian duke to prepare a library, a task that took 14 years to complete. These magnificent books, said Da Portici, were "beautiful volumes all bound in crimson and silver and all written with the pen, for the Duke would be ashamed to possess a single printed book."

Eventually, however, printed books came to be accepted by everyone, and as early as 1515 all the Greek manuscripts available in Europe had been printed. By now, of course, millions of books by ancient authors have been printed, in dozens of different languages all over the world. We may, therefore, hope that this heritage will never be lost, as it was lost before, whatever disasters may strike humanity in the future.

# VI THE DEAD SEA SCROLLS

Our study of ancient scrolls and other forms of writing has covered a time span of thousands of years, from the first crude signs and symbols scratched onto stone tablets to beautiful illuminated Bibles written on fine parchment. It has included accounts of many interesting examples of ancient writings that have been preserved or rediscovered in modern times, such as the Codex Sinaiticus, the *Keter-ha-Torah*, the Greek Anthology, and the papyrus manuscripts of ancient Egypt. But we have saved the most famous of those stories for last, so that it can be told more fully than the others. It concerns one of the most recent of all discoveries and one of the most ancient groups of manuscripts ever found: the Dead Sea Scrolls.

On the border between Israel and Jordan, about 50 miles east of the Mediterranean Sea, there is a great valley over 200 miles long, running north to south through a mountainous desert. The Jordan River runs south down this valley for about 65 miles and empties into one of the lowest and saltiest bodies of water in the world — the Dead Sea.

The Dead Sea itself is surrounded by rugged mountains and rocky cliffs, and there are steep valleys that run down to its shores. Along the steep sides of many of these valleys are caves large enough for people to live in. In ancient times these caves served as hiding places and emergency shelters.

The desert country near the Dead Sea is so dry that an average of only three inches of rain falls each year, only one inch per year more than California's Death Valley. During periods of trouble in ancient times, the inhabitants of this land would often hide their valuable possessions in the caves around the Dead Sea; because the land was so dry, these possessions simply did not decay. Some of the ancient writers mention that very old copies of the Bible were found long ago near the town of Jericho (five miles from the Dead Sea), but these stories were not taken seriously by modern scholars. As we shall see, however, the scholars eventually had good reason to change their minds.

## The Discovery of the Scrolls

One day in 1947, a boy named Muhammad edh-Dibh (in Arabic, "the Wolf") was tending his flock of goats in the desert wilderness southwest of Jericho, not far from the shores of the Dead Sea. Muhammad belonged to a group of people known as Beduins, desert tribesmen who live mostly in tents and who still wander throughout the Near East with their camels, horses, sheep, and goats. Muhammad and his flock were climbing a hillside at a place called Qumran, near the ruins of an old Roman fort. In the cliffside across from the ruin, he noticed the opening of a cave, and he threw a stone into its dark mouth. Instead of the simple clatter of stone against stone, Muhammad was surprised to hear the crashing sound of pottery jars breaking. When he returned to the Beduin camp, he told the others what he had heard, and soon the boy and a number of his tribesmen returned to the cave to investigate. When they entered the cave, they found several large pottery jars containing parchment scrolls that had been carefully wrapped in linen. The linen itself had then been covered with pitch (the sticky sap of certain evergreen trees), and as a result the manuscripts themselves were fairly well preserved.

Not knowing what to make of this strange discovery, the Beduins showed some of the scrolls to a dealer in the nearby town of Bethlehem who bought and sold ancient objects. The dealer agreed to look for someone who might want to buy the scrolls. He took some of them to Jerusalem, where he showed them to some people he knew there. At first, the scholars in Jerusalem were puzzled by these strange-looking scrolls. Since they had never seen scrolls like these, some thought that the Beduins' discovery was a hoax and that the manuscripts were just forgeries.

A few of the scholars, however, including Professor Sukenik of the Hebrew University at Jerusalem, recognized them as authentic ancient manuscripts. Professor Sukenik was able to acquire some of the scrolls, and the rest were purchased by a Patriarch of the Syrian Catholic Church named Mar Samuel. Mar Samuel was uncertain about the real value of the scrolls, so he consulted a scholar from the American School

*Right:* Jars in which some of the Dead Sea Scrolls were found

of Oriental Research in Jerusalem, allowing him to take photographs of the manuscripts. Some of these photographs were seen by American scholars, who recognized one of them — a scroll of Isaiah — as the oldest surviving manuscript of any book of the Bible. It was prepared during the second century B.C., which made it more than 1,000 years older than the oldest manuscript of the Hebrew Bible previously known! Before long, the American scholars published exact copies of the contents of the scrolls that Mar Samuel had purchased, so that other scholars might be able to study them as well. The scrolls purchased by Professor Sukenik were published a few years later.

By this time, dealers and collectors were willing to pay high prices for even small parts of these Dead Sea Scrolls. In the end, the scrolls came to be worth about $2.50 per square inch. As soon as the Beduins realized how valuable these scrolls really were, they began to search other caves in the vicinity of the Dead Sea, hoping to find manuscripts. Scholars also began searching for more scrolls themselves, and soon the search for ancient manuscripts had turned into a race between the Beduins and the scholars. With their superior knowledge of the countryside, their better physical condition, and the greater amount of time they could devote to the search, the Beduins eventually won this race for discovery. In all, 11 caves turned out to contain ancient scrolls. The scholars discovered six of these caves, but — except for some curious copper scrolls — these six caves yielded only scraps of manuscripts. Three of the caves discovered by the Beduins, however, contained many important scrolls.

## The Contents of the Scrolls

Almost all of the Dead Sea Scrolls are written on parchment; the only exceptions are the copper scrolls and some texts written on papyrus. Two kinds of ink were used in preparing the manuscripts. One is the common ink made of lampblack; the scrolls written with this ink are fairly well preserved. The other kind of ink contains a metallic substance that has corroded the parchment. Some of these manuscripts are so badly corroded that the lines of writing themselves have disappeared, leaving intact only the blank strips of parchment that had been between the lines.

The Hebrew script in which most of these scrolls were written is of the type used around the time of Christ. But a few copies of the Book of Leviticus are written in a much older script, one that is still used by the Samaritans, an ancient religious group. In one copy of the Book of Exodus, red ink was used to mark the lines for writing, and the headings of the various sections are written in red. Another interesting detail is that the sacred name of God was written in the old script inside a square. This name, represented by the English consonants YHWH, is pronounced *Adonai* in Hebrew, but no one actually knows how it should be pronounced. Apparently, the name was so sacred that the ancient Hebrews dared not say it aloud, and its correct pronunciation has been lost.

There were two different kinds of writings found in the caves at Qumran. One kind consisted of manuscripts of various books of the Bible. The scholars found parts of every single book of the Old Testament Bible except the Book of Esther. Some of the books have been completely preserved, and there were several copies of certain books — such as Isaiah and Psalms — that were used by the ancient inhabitants of Qumran for their community prayers. One cave, in fact, contained a total of 54 copies of only four different books. There were also manuscripts of two books of the Bible — Daniel and Ecclesiastes — that

had been written only a century after the ancient Hebrews composed them.

The other kind of writings found in the caves was composed by the people who lived at Qumran. One group of writings describes the rules and regulations that should govern all forms of behavior. The first section of writings in this group deals with the rules to be followed by the members of the community. Another section describes the way the community thought all Jews should live. The last section contains the various blessings to be said on the important ceremonial occasions that the community observed.

A second group of writings describes an imaginary war between the "Sons of Light," who represent the forces of good, and the "Sons of Darkness," who represent the forces of evil. Scholars believe that the Sons of Light signified the members of the community, while the Sons of Darkness were intended to signify their enemies. In the end, of course, the Sons of Light are victorious over the Sons of Darkness.

The third group of writings is called the Thanksgiving Scroll. This scroll contains a number of poems written by members of the community, expressing their gratitude and devotion to God.

A final group of writings consists of a number of copper scrolls, which were mentioned at the very beginning of this book. These scrolls describe a fantastic list of treasures that were hidden in various parts of the Holy Land, especially in Jerusalem. The Qumran community probably used copper to make sure that the scrolls would be preserved, but no one knows whether the treasures listed on it are real or imaginary. A number of people have already searched for these treasures, but not a trace of them has ever been found.

As you have probably guessed, the people who lived at Qumran in ancient times were not ordinary villagers. (For one thing, ordinary people of those times did not read and write, much less compose long and complicated descriptions of the rules they thought people should live by.) The Qumran community was a very devout religious sect that had arisen in the Holy Land during the second century B.C. Almost everything we know about this sect comes from the scrolls which they left behind. Until the scrolls were discovered in 1947 no one ever suspected there had been a religious community living at Qumran.

## The Dead Sea Sect

The Dead Sea Sect seems to have been founded by one man, a religious leader whose name has been lost. In the writings of the sect, he is referred to as the "Teacher of Righteousness" or the "Master of Justice." According to the scrolls, this leader was executed by a wicked priest, and the members of the sect fled to Damascus, Syria.

During the last years of the second century B.C., the members of the sect settled at Qumran. The monastery that they built there has now been excavated by archaeologists. It contained a large group of rooms, including a room for eating meals together, a scriptorium where the scrolls were copied, and a number of pools that had once been filled with water from the surrounding hills and mountains. These pools were used for ritual baths during religious ceremonies; the members of the sect believed strongly in ritual purity. Although quite a large number of rooms have been unearthed, they are probably only a small part of the original monastery.

The Dead Sea Sect was organized into two groups: an inner circle and an outer circle. The inner circle consisted only of grown men. They were the principal members and leaders of the community, and they were required to obey all of the special rules written down in the scrolls. The inner circle was divided into three ranks. The highest rank consisted of the priests, who were in charge of the spiritual life of the community. Next came the levites, who assisted the priests in their duties. The lowest rank of the inner circle consisted of ordinary members, who were allowed to take part in the ceremonial gatherings and to share the common meals with the priests and levites.

The inner circle of the sect lived largely as a communal society; its members believed that all property should be owned by everyone in common. When a man became a member of the inner circle, he had to hand over all of his possessions to a special official, who was in charge of all community property. A man joining the inner circle did not immediately become a full member. Before he could be fully accepted, he had to spend two years learning the rules of proper behavior and demonstrating that he would be a worthwhile member of the community. Members of the inner circle who did not obey the rules might be expelled from the community. The sect regarded this expulsion as a kind of spiritual death.

The members of the outer circle, which included the women and children of the community, were not required to obey such strict rules. They did not practice communal ownership and therefore did not have to hand over all of their possessions to the community.

Qumran served as the headquarters of the Dead Sea Sect during most of the first century B.C., although during the reign of King Herod the Great (in the last 30 years before the birth of Christ) the sect may have moved to Jerusalem. Herod died in 4 B.C., however, and shortly after his death the sect moved back to the monastery at Qumran. They lived there until the year A.D. 68, when the Romans destroyed the monastery.

*Beliefs of the Dead Sea Sect*

The people of Qumran believed that God had determined the fate of the entire world — and of every person in it — from the very beginning of creation. They believed that when the world ended only a select few would be saved, while most of humanity would be condemned for all eternity. Naturally, the members of the Dead Sea Sect considered themselves a part of that select few. Finally, they believed that the earth was the scene of a great struggle between God — whose side they were on — and the

Devil, whom they called "Belial."

The people of Qumran were Jews, but they did not accept the authority of the religious leaders who held power in the Holy Land at that time. They considered the high priests appointed by King Herod to be un-authorized, and they did not believe that the temple in Jerusalem was sacred or even legitimate. Moreover, the Dead Sea Sect followed its own calendar, which differed from that of the other Jews. As a result the sect observed religious holidays on different days from the rest of the Jewish people. On the days that the sect considered holy, the rest of the Jews would be at work. But when most Jews celebrated their holidays, the members of the Dead Sea Sect would be working. This difference must have caused much antagonism between the sect and the other Jews. Thus the sect found it easier to live apart from the rest of the Jewish people. This is why the monastery was built out in the desert wilder-ness: in that lonely place, the com-munity could live more easily by its own rules.

## Studying the Dead Sea Scrolls

Ever since the Dead Sea Scrolls were discovered, scholars have been trying to understand what relation-ships existed between the Dead Sea Sect and some of the other important people of that period in history. One of the most intriguing of these ques-tions concerns the sect's relationship to Jesus and to the early Christians. There are many similarities between the teachings of the Christians and the beliefs of the Dead Sea Sect. Moreover, both groups practiced communal ownership of material possessions and ate their meals to-gether. Even some of the poems in the Thanksgiving Scroll are similar to some of the early Christian doc-trines, including Jesus' Sermon on the Mount. It is almost certain that there was some contact between the Dead Sea Sect and the followers of Jesus, and Jesus himself may have known of the religious community at Qumran. It is even possible that he visited the community, since John the Baptist preached and performed baptisms at the Jordan River, not far from the monastery itself. Jesus himself may have lived in the sur-rounding mountains during his 40-day retreat into the wilderness.

Although some people have sug-gested that Jesus may have been the real founder of the sect or that the early Christians were once members of the sect itself, most scholars agree that these theories could not possibly be true. But the people of Qumran and the early Christians probably knew of each other's existence, and they may very well have borrowed some religious ideas and inspiration from each other. In time, however, the two movements grew apart. Christianity developed into one of the most powerful religious movements in the history of civilization, while the Dead Sea Sect quickly disappeared, leaving behind only a number of ancient scrolls. If these scrolls had not been found, the Qumran community would have been forgotten forever. As it is, our discovery of the Dead Sea Scrolls has made the sect seem more important than it really was. The Dead Sea Sect consisted of only a few thousand individuals out of a population of millions of Jews, and its effect on history was small.

The discovery of the Dead Sea Scrolls encouraged people to search for more written records in the vicinity of the Dead Sea. In time, other ancient writings, written in other periods of history, were found in the caves of nearby valleys. One

One of the Thanksgiving Scrolls

A 2000-year-old land lease, written in the name of Bar Kochba

group of manuscripts contains letters and documents of the Jewish rebel army led by Bar Kochba that fought against the Romans between A.D. 132 and 135. These manuscripts tell us a great deal about the languages and military history of ancient Palestine. Among these writings are the personal papers of a woman named Babata, who fled from her home during the rebellion. Babata was a relative of one of the rebel leaders, and she fled to the safety of the caves he occupied. From the documents she brought with her, it is possible to reconstruct her whole life history. The story of Babata's life contains information about the customs and laws of those times that is of enormous interest to archaeologists and historians.

Another group of writings was found in a cave northwest of Jericho. Although these are among the oldest documents ever discovered in the Holy Land, they are written on papyrus. They date from the fourth century B.C., when a group of Samaritans fled from their homes, fearing death at the hands of Greek soldiers. These documents have only begun to be studied.

Before we can judge the importance of the many ancient manuscripts that have been found in the region of the Dead Sea, we must remember that scholars have only begun the enormous task of studying them. It will take many years to learn what their exact meanings are, after all the different possible interpretations have been considered. Fi-

A letter by Bar Kochba

A leather bag containing the letters of Bar Kochba

nally, we must remember that these ancient writings, priceless though they may be, give us only a small glimpse of what happened in the past. Through them we can see many of the tiny details of what a few individuals were doing. But from these details historians attempt to understand what entire societies were doing and what whole periods of history must have been like. This is difficult yet exciting work, and it requires knowledge, patience, and imagination.

So little information has survived from ancient times that the historians' job is somewhat like trying to make out the picture in a puzzle when most of the pieces have been lost. The few remaining pieces may torment us with frustration, because there are often not enough of them to outline the original picture. Without them, however, we would have nothing, and the past would be a complete mystery. The discovery of ancient manuscripts has made it possible to understand some of this mystery, and each new discovery brings the past more clearly into view.

# GLOSSARY

| | |
|---|---|
| *album* | A whitened board used for displaying public notices. |
| *anthology* | A collection of excerpts from the writings of several authors. |
| *Book of the Dead* | A manuscript placed in the tombs of rich Egyptian commoners to serve as a guide in the afterlife. |
| *Byblos* | A seaport of ancient Phoenicia from which the Phoenicians shipped papyrus to Greece. |
| *codex* (1) | A group of wooden tablets fastened together like a book. |
| *codex* (2) | Sheet of writing material folded into the shape of a book. |
| *Codex Sinaiticus* | The oldest copy of the Christian version of the Bible known to exist, written in Greek in the fourth century A.D. |
| *cuneiform* | Wedge-shaped symbols or characters used in writing on clay tablets. |
| *Dead Sea Sect* | The members of the religious community at Qumran, who withdrew to their desert monastery near the Dead Sea to pursue a life of spiritual purity and religious devotion. |
| *digest* | A greatly shortened version of a body of writing, containing only the most important information. |

*diploma*                     A certificate of citizenship, given by the Romans to honorably discharged soldiers.

*emending*                    The science of improving or correcting a text that was not copied perfectly and contains errors.

*Greek Anthology*             A collection of ancient Greek poems, begun in the first century B.C. and expanded during the Middle Ages.

*hieroglyphics*               The picture-writing of the ancient Egyptians.

*illumination*                The art of illustrating or decorating a manuscript.

*Keter-ha-Torah*              One of the oldest and most beautiful Torah scrolls in existence, dating from the 10th century A.D.

*Massoretes*                  Hebrew scribes and scholars of the Middle Ages, who established a correct text of the Hebrew Bible.

*Middle Ages*                 The period from the fall of Rome to the beginning of the Renaissance, roughly from 500 to 1300 A.D.

*millennium*                  A thousand years. "During the first millennium B.C." means "during the first 1,000 years before Christ."

*ostraca*                     Fragments of pottery used as writing materials.

*palimpsest*                  A manuscript, usually of parchment, consisting of an original text that has been erased and a new text that has been copied onto the original pages.

*papyrus*                     Writing material similar to paper, made in Egypt from the stems of the papyrus plant.

*parchment*                   Untanned sheepskin, goatskin, or calfskin, used as a writing material.

*Pergamon*                    A small kingdom in northwestern Turkey, famous for its fine parchment and its great library.

*potsherd*                    Fragment of a broken pottery vessel.

| | |
|---|---|
| *pumice* | A light, powdery, spongelike rock used for polishing. |
| *Qumran* | A place west of Jerusalem, near the Dead Sea, where the Dead Sea Scrolls were found. |
| *Renaissance* | The artistic and scientific awakening of European society, beginning in Italy in the 14th century. |
| *roll* | A rolled-up strip of parchment or papyrus; a scroll. |
| *scribe* | A person who copies manuscripts and documents for a living. |
| *scriptorium* | A room in a monastery where manuscripts and records were written or copied. |
| *scroll* | A strip of writing material, usually rolled into the shape of a tube. |
| *stylus* | A sharp writing instrument, used for inscribing words onto wax or clay tablets. |
| *tablet* | A slab of some solid material with a flat surface used for writing. |
| *Talmud* | The traditional laws and teachings of the Jewish people, including the commentaries upon them by generations of Jewish scholars. |
| *tannin* | A chemical extract from tree bark, used for making leather by tanning animal skins. |
| *text* | A piece of writing; the exact wording of a written work. |
| *Torah* | The parchment scroll used in synagogues during Jewish services. It contains the first five books of the Bible. |
| *vellum* | A fine grade of parchment made from the skin of calves or kids. |

# INDEX

MICHAEL AVI-YONAH is a professor of classical archaeology and history of art at the Hebrew University in Jerusalem. Born in Eastern Europe, Dr. Avi-Yonah came to Israel in 1921. After receiving his Ph.D. from University College in London, he began a career of research and writing in the field of archaeology. Dr. Avi-Yonah has headed major archaeological excavations in Israel at sites such as Masada, Caesarea, and Jerusalem. He had written books on a variety of subjects, ranging from mosaics pavements in Palestine to the history of the Holy Land. Dr. Avi-Yonah and his wife, a talented artist, make their home in Jerusalem.

RICHARD L. CURRIER received his A.B. and Ph.D. degrees in anthropology from the University of California at Berkeley. He has done field work in Mexico and in Greece and has taught anthropology both at Berkeley and at the University of Minnesota. Dr. Currier now devotes full time to writing and research.